Modern Trends in Hospitality Industry

MODERN TRENDS IN HOSPITALITY INDUSTRY

DR. Raj Kumar Singh
D.H.C.T. Mgmt. (W.B.)
P.G.D.B. Mgmt. (U.P.)
C.F.N. (Delhi)
MHCIMA (London)
Ph.D. (Management)
Director
'SAMS' Institute of Hotel Management,
Varanasi

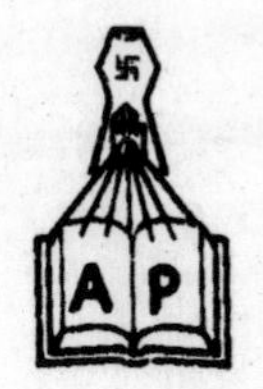

AMAN PUBLICATIONS
NEW DELHI (INDIA)

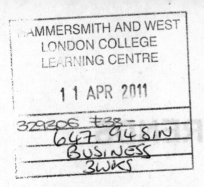

Published by
Rajiv Jain for Aman Publications
LG-4A, Ganpati Bhawan,
4675-B/21, Ansari Road,
Darya Ganj, Delhi - 110002
PH: 23255012, 23282127
E-mail: sshjbs@yahoo.com

[The responsibility for the facts stated, conclusions reached etc. is entirely that of the Author. The publisher is not responsible for them, whatsoever.]

First Edition 2006
ISBN-81-8204-017-5 (PB)

SOLE DISTRIBUTOR
JINDAL BOOK SERVICES
LG-4A, Ganpati Bhawan,
4675-B/21, Ansari Road,
Darya Ganj, Delhi - 110002

Laser Typesetting by:
S.M. Graphics, Delhi,

Printed by:
NCT Printers & Publishers , Delhi, India

Preface

The hospitality industry is defined as the activity of providing lodging, food and beverage, and recreational services, which include but are not limited to hotels, motels, clubs, casinos, restaurants, recreation facilities, tourism, cruise lines, and theme parks. A multi-billion dollar industry, hospitality is one of largest and rapidly growing industry in the world. This industry is closely linked to the tourism industry, as a majority of consumers for services within the hospitality industry comes from domestic and international tourists.

The hospitality industry has gone through tremendous change over the last decade. Some changes have been dictated by technological advances, such as the shift from mainframe access via dumb terminals and green screens, to the current emphasis on above-property applications leveraging data from a single source. Other changes, such as the increased use of the internet spawned a plethora of new opportunities along with new intermediaries. And, of course, the economy and geopolitical events have impacted the industry.

This book offers a comprehensive analysis of modern trends in hospitality industry. Well organised and easy to use, this book is an important training tool for those embarking on careers in hospitality.

Contents

1

Modern Technologies in Hospitality Industry

In today's competitive business environment, hospitality industry executives are faced with abundant challenges, one of the most important being how to lower overhead while revenues are increasing. This has become exceptionally vital for the large 'chain' hotel companies that deal with significant competitions form the independent hotel management companies. In recent times, the hospitality industry has gained from tourists' popularity and substantial overseas investment, enabling the construction of many new international standard hotels and resorts, renovation of existing inns, taverns and restaurants and extended travel operations.

This time for hotel industry to gain momentum of providing 'excellent service' and one of the tools of providing excellent service is through training. There have been a lot of papers arguing some imperative components should be aware of future environment particularly when the hospitality industry moves into the year 2000. Professional bodies have also joined with current research in encouraging the hospitality industry to very much concerned and focused on the customer relationship, how this relationship can be measured in terms of satisfaction and value.

Concept of Electronic Business

For those operating within the physical world, the concept of electronic business or "e-business" may appear to be of limited significance. But such an assumption could be costly. The financial markets are making massive investments in the companies that deliver Internet technologies, content and related products and services, and the corporate world is now moving toward e-business offerings at a rapid clip. On the business-to-business (b-to-b) front, e-business is projected to grow enormously in the United States over the next several years, with business-to-consumer (b-to-c) trade not as big, but growing just as fast.

E-business is rewriting the economic rules globally for every industry-including hospitality, travel and leisure. Indeed, it's important to recognise that we are now operating in what has been described as the "new economy," as global trends drive change, including globalisation, consolidation, convergence, technology and communications. Even more, it is clear that the underlying sources of value are also changing. Use of intangible assets such as information, brands, customers, relationships and networks distinguish the most successful companies in the world.

Role of Internet

It is clear that the Internet is having a huge impact on how we conduct our lives and our businesses. And it arrived virtually overnight. In the United States, for example, it took 38 years for television to get into 50 million homes. For the Internet, it took just five years. And for those U.S. consumers that are online, four out of five believe that the Internet is a more important invention than television. Of these same online consumers, close to six in 10 prefer e-mail to paper mail for business correspondence and over one in four check their e-mail while on vacation.

The Internet is also changing the customer relationship-undermining and redirecting customer attention to new sellers of products and services and away from their traditional relationships. And as this occurs, the traditional approaches that hospitality businesses have taken to distribution are all being affected. From reservations taken over the Internet, which are projected to more than double to 9% of volume over the next year, to the declining role of the travel agent. This occurs as so-called "infomediaries" provide information and access, and software robots troll the activity online to develop matches between buyers and sellers, analysing complex patterns and looking for trends for marketers to capitalise upon.

As for the infomediaries, we can expect some of these to move into the transactions business and continue the process of disintermediation. For some hospitality companies, it may be best to join this new competition, particularly if it cannot be beaten at its own game. The reality today is that the balance of power is shifting from sellers to buyers and in so doing it makes the importance of delivering high-quality service, convenience and value for money ever more compelling. The Internet has clearly levelled the playing field by making price information broadly available to the consumer.

Internet business models affect product and services offerings, pricing, distribution and customer service, as well as long-term information capabilities. As a consequence, some hospitality suppliers will inevitably feed different tranches of their inventory through the various channels at their disposal-including the Internet, travel management organisations, destination packagers and the like.

Today's fast-paced world produces ever more stress, and consumers want information and they want it fast. And if hospitality companies and travel providers don't deliver convenience, somebody else inevitably will. They also want to be wired up to the rest of the world-at home, in their office and especially when they travel. And for hoteliers trying to cope with in-room technologies and the delivery of high-speed Internet access, we will soon be seeing more integration of network communication and entertainment products to further complicate or liberate our lives, depending on your point of view. Customers are also looking for consistency-a simple concept, but central to whether a brand has value or not. And in the emerging networked world, aligning the value propositions of alliance partners and ensuring a seamless and consistent experience will only be as good as the weakest link in the chain.

New Business Rules

Within this new economy, the operating environment for hospitality companies is changing. There are new rules of conduct, new relationships and new criteria for success, along with a new set of metrics. In such an era there are certain traits to business behaviour that will distinguish success from failure. At this stage in the new economy's evolution, these traits would appear to include speed, agility and flexibility.

Speed is necessary to get to market early with a first-mover advantage that assures early adoption by an increasingly fickle, restless and frequently disloyal customer. Such speed is imperative as so-called "start-up" companies come to dominate their chosen niche in extremely short periods of time, frequently preempting the opportunity for those too slow to react.

Agility is required to be able to respond to competitive threats by not only those we know and can monitor, but also unseen competitors. These latter competitors may not even exist as yet, but as they emerge, they may quickly disintermediate established customer relationships.

And, finally, flexibility is needed to reorganise the established models of business and all of the related processes, and adapt the organisation in organic fashion to a new environment in whatever form it takes.

For business executives at large, one of the most compelling changes that has confronted them in recent years is the potential for e-business. But while the significance of these new media are all too apparent, the business solutions required to capitalise on opportunities they offer are unfortunately not. For most hospitality executives, the essential frame of reference has been a geocentric one where real estate and geography have been the big drivers in a physical world-buildings, dots on maps, markets served, chains.

In tomorrow's world, these concepts will require some fundamental adjustments to provide for market "spaces" rather than "places" as the nature of relationships between hotel businesses, their customers, their suppliers and their alliance partners go through rapid and constant change. As these changes occur, the new economy's business leaders must quickly learn the new rules of the game and adjust their approaches accordingly. And the most successful among us will align key processes around the Internet, build corporate intelligence automatically, create integrated value chains and develop new processes to deal with an ever-changing set of circumstances.

Human Capital

Supporting the changes in the new economy will be a vast pool of talented human capital anxious to bring new ideas and new technologies to bear on the traditional ways of doing business and, in doing so, steadily increase the pace of productivity improvement. And if the hospitality industry is to respond to this coming reality, it will need to address some of its most vexing challenges-particularly those relating to the recruitment, training and development of human capital. The human capital inventory for an e-business will require entrepreneurship, as well as visionary leadership, strength in sales and marketing and commitment to customer relationship management. The organisational bias will need to be toward creativity and risk-taking, and away from dependency on analysis and procedures.

In addition to the human capital challenge, many of today's legacy organisations are better structured to work in the old economy, but are considerably less aligned for many activities in the "new." The cultural challenges may in fact be no less daunting than those presented by some of the technological ones. For large organisations attempting a major shift in orientation, the presence of a significant culture may turn out to be quite a hindrance.

In some industries, profits are made on spare parts and maintenance rather than on mainstream products. In the new economy, this business model replicated in the hospitality industry. And for those companies that discount or give away products such as hotel rooms in order to sell linked services, they surely will be redefining the meaning of hospitality. They will also be marketing an array of hospitality and leisure products and services to a customer base that is no longer satisfied with the traditional ways of making such purchases.

Hospitality businesses that traditionally provided room, board, management and marketing may need to rethink their roles in the new economy, particularly as services become more valuable than products. With the rapid growth of "infomediaries" and their facilitation of transactions, hospitality businesses may need to redefine themselves in order to prosper in an increasingly electronic world where one-to-one customisation is the order of the day. But for those contemplating repositioning their companies in an e-business environment, it will be necessary to focus on the current value proposition of the business and determine how it might be reformatted or enhanced to ensure success in the new setting.

In Arthur Andersen's recently published global survey of technology, *Hospitality 2000: The Technology*, we addressed some of the issues that the industry is facing. These included the closed nature of our technology architectures, the way in which we collect information on our customers, our investments in Internet, intranet and extranet technologies, and our adoption of electronic commerce. The results are not especially encouraging and suggest an industry still relatively slow to adapt to e-business.

Only 39% of the industry's Web sites, for example, can handle reservations on a real-time basis, and even fewer still (19%), collect customer information. At the same time, just 22% are using "push" marketing programs and a distinct minority (just 19%), have extranets to suppliers or customers. But these adoption rates are nonetheless projected to grow and we should, therefore, expect our industry's leaders to be far more attuned to the needs of an e-business environment in the years to come.

As information technology (IT) is used to facilitate a company's entry into the world of electronic commerce, our industry's leadership will also need to overcome a natural tendency to be disappointed by the role of IT in achieving competitive advantage. For many years IT was seen as a mechanism to support back office finance and accounting functions. In the future, it inevitably will be one of the principal drivers of value creation in the new economy. But we should not be mislead by IT-in e-business, it will be the strategy, not the technology that will make the difference between success and failure. But having the strategy in place is only the first step. It must be linked to every part of the business.

Planning Strategy for E-business

With the costs of playing in the e-business world escalating rapidly, hospitality executives should consider the four phases of what might be called the "E-Business Lifecycle." The first of these-E-Business Strategy Development and Planning-must address the market and competitive context, articulate the vision and opportunity, outline the strategy and the business case, and identify the risks. In recent years, we have frequently seen hospitality businesses put up a Web site on the Internet and consider this an e-business strategy. But without a strategy for this new form of commerce and the business planning process to drive it, such reactionary approaches stand little chance for success.

Once the plan is in place, an e-business design phase can commence to address site design, lay out the business architecture, identify the technical infrastructure, plan for performance, availability and capacity, and deal with tax issues and enterprise security. Following the design phase, E-Business implementation will prepare for the launch with training and change enablement, implementation and integration, testing and roll-out. Once in place, E-Business Operations will need to be supported by IT and audit services, Web site activity analysis and Web site maintenance. Finally, measurement systems will need to be established to monitor performance.

As industry executives embark on this e-business lifecycle, they will need in the first stage to clearly establish the business case for investing in new technologies, systems and organisations by addressing both the cost reduction and revenue enhancement benefits. On the revenue side, there are a number of factors to consider. These include the company's ability to identify and recruit the most valuable customers; the ability to seamlessly cross-sell the company's products and services, as well as those of alliance partners; the ability to retain valuable customers and reduce attrition (especially relevant in a world of questionable brand loyalty); and finally, when and how to eliminate costly and unnecessary discounts through revenue optimisation.

In this kind of environment, the property management system will no longer hold sway as the center of the hospitality universe, but will become just one in a series of customer touch-points that will increasingly include the Internet. These touch-points will ultimately need to be fully integrated into a customer information system supported by sophisticated data warehousing and data mining technologies.

Adding to the industry's costs in this portrait of the future is the cost of grafting e-business technologies onto the industry's legacy systems. At a certain stage, it may make sense to start from scratch and ensure that every system is Web-enabled. This would allow a total interface for a high-growth e-business, thereby maximising the customer relationship management opportunities that it presents.

As to the role of the Internet, its comprehensive reach and ubiquitous nature has already ensured its central place in the new economy. But how should we evaluate whether an Internet application is deserving of our attention? Firstly, productivity on the Internet in the years to come will be vastly improved by much higher bandwidth than is currently in place. And with higher bandwidth will come applications that can benefit from such extra capacity delivering tightly focused and reliable content to an increasingly sophisticated and demanding e-customer. If an Internet application is to succeed in the future, it will therefore need to be designed to capitalise on this coming reality.

Secondly, an Internet application needs to form a community of some sort because without a sense of place, albeit of the virtual sort participants will not have that all-important sense of belonging. And as with the industrial revolution, which drew a disparate population to centers of economic activity, so will such "intranet communities" grow in value as their populations increase in size and their economic product expands.

For larger businesses that form such communities, they are developing new revenue sources and are reinventing their relationships with customers, employees, suppliers and partners. Smaller companies intent on participating in this new environment, may need to be content as a participant in an established community, rather than trying to take on the creation of a community itself. It is better, perhaps, to be one of many players in a successful space than struggling to establish an identity in a world surrounded by also-rans.

Whether large or small, community developers and marketers of the virtual sort will have to recognise that what may have appeared cool in the physical world to generations brought up in the old economy will not work in the world of e-business. Being cool and staying that way in order to get and keep attention will remain a constant challenge, especially for those keen to nurture a younger generation of travellers brought up on MTV and the Web.

Finally, the successful Internet application needs to improve service while reducing transaction costs, particularly as the balance of power in the buy/sell relationship continues its inexorable migration from sellers to buyers. Service improvement strategies will be nothing new for hospitality businesses, but it is noteworthy that service (rather than on-time delivery, price or other concerns) is the top factor that encourages return e-business. This must be an area of focus since the current growth of e-business appears destined to outpace the supporting infrastructure and its related service at least over the short term. But as hospitality executives know, delivering good service can be expensive.

Scaling the types of service response to the circumstances is a growing need, but one that can be modulated if the value of each customer can be distinguished and the response adjusted accordingly. In considering the opportunities in hospitality e-business, industry leaders should take stock of the dynamics that are occurring in the new economy and plan accordingly. It is probably easy to dismiss the e-business world as a playground for others with products and services that are more obviously applicable. .

Hospitality eProcurement

eProcurement is a direct outgrowth of that capability. As a global network using standardised protocols and universal connectivity, the Internet opens the door for businesses to develop international marketplaces for their products and services. Not only does the Internet facilitate the sharing of information, it simplifies the process for the end-user as well, and reduces infrastructure and transaction costs.

The shared nature of the Internet distributes the infrastructure costs across large groups of potential customers, suppliers and others. That means businesses of any size can gain access for a variety of purposes.

Distributors or suppliers can build revenue while also realising reduced customer contact costs. Rather than maintaining multiple sales contact systems, suppliers need to have just one connection to the Internet. What is the real potential for hospitality companies?

eProcurement will have a positive impact on business functions and processes for those organisations that fully take advantage of these capabilities. Buyers, for example, have a growing amount of information available to identify the suppliers with whom they want to do business. eProcurement facilitates the aggregation of small purchases, thereby making the order process more efficient and cost effective. And it minimises the need for intermediaries between the supplier and buyer.

Using digitised processes, the procurement process is engineered in concert with an all-electronic design and implementation of the infrastructure required to source, supply, manage and control services. It is one of the most important of business-to-business (B2B) functions. eProcurement solutions were initially launched by companies such as Ariba, Inc., which developed corporate procurement systems for global 2000 companies to give their employees access to vendors electronically. Though effective, these applications centering on "buy-side" solutions were inherently expensive and time-consuming to implement.

The new generation of eProcurement is more revolutionary. Today, digital marketplaces create Internet portals to serve multiple buyers and sellers in the exchange of goods and services. These new ventures are levelling the playing field for both buyers and suppliers, giving smaller companies and those around the world ready access, using a Web browser, to opportunities once available primarily to larger companies in North America.

Marketplace Models

The development of eProcurement offerings, hospitality companies will benefit by understanding the emerging digital marketplace models. There are currently two dominant models:

Industry-specific marketplaces: Organisations with domain expertise in a particular industry—or industry "vertical" in the language of the new economy—launch these exchanges. These market-places support commerce specific to an industry as they seek to aggregate buyers and sellers to reduce transaction costs. Their competitive advantage is based on a unique understanding of industry inefficiencies. Instill bundles eProcurement services to improve control and management of foodservice purchasing, offers a consolidated purchase information service for monitoring contract compliance and capturing rebates, provides market intelligence to manufacturers, and creates an online community and marketplace for small chains and independent operators to improve their operating and financial performance.

Horizontal marketplaces: These exchanges provide a vehicle for many types of buyers and sellers to advertise, share content, bid on products, participate in auctions and manage their supply chains. Such marketplace sites serve a wide range of disparate industries and/or provide them with access to horizontal applications.

Unlike the original eProcurement systems, which generally provided static catalogues and limited sourcing capability, these new digital marketplaces use dynamic pricing models—primarily auctions or exchanges - which are based on demand. Horizontal marketplaces have multiple revenue streams, the most common of which come from advertising on sites. Many of these marketplaces also generate revenues in the form of commissions charged to sellers participating in auctions.

Storefront sales to sellers can be an additional source of revenue for such marketplaces.

Vertical marketplaces have similar revenue sources, although they are able to command higher advertising fees due to the detailed information they can collect on concentrated groups of members and subscribers. Additionally, some of them also generate revenues by charging subscription fees to access their focused content and product data. In contrast to vertical marketplaces, horizontal marketplaces face challenges specific to their broad mission. Based on the need to appeal to diverse industries, these marketplaces must satisfy the product, service and content needs of their varied buyers and members, and may be fighting an uphill battle in doing so.

Some companies have been successful using this model, but they have had to invest in expensive domain experts to develop the compelling offerings typically available in a vertical marketplace. The diversity of the industries served by horizontal marketplaces, however, can be useful in reducing risk in the event of limited penetration in a particular vertical. A hybrid marketplace model is beginning to emerge with the advantage of leveraging the strengths of both models. In this model several contiguous verticals are represented in a marketplace. These contiguous verticals can be grouped according to the similar products and services used by all, yet still maintain the content and other offerings unique to each.

Global eBusiness will be fueled by the ability to track the movement of trade goods at any point along the supply chain. Ships transporting goods from Latin America to North America, for example, might be quickly redirected to Europe in the event that bids were greater in other locations. Such flexibility in real-time pricing would greatly minimise reliance on fixed prices. The implications for various segments of the hospitality industry in the following points:

Brands

— Established brands can leverage their relationships, experience, knowledge and purchasing power to reengineer corporate purchasing efforts for improved efficiency.

— These players can develop (or partner with vendors and/or with competitors) private, secure, customised sites for employees to purchase products and services from approved vendors. Real-time inventory management and accounting then becomes possible.

— The major brands can also take control of the procurement process by minimising "maverick" purchases and monitoring adherence to approved vendor lists, ensuring their employees adhere to quality standards.

Management Companies and Independents

— These companies will gain access to rebates traditionally only available to larger companies based on aggregated demand.

— The buying power of hotels outside North America, which have had little clout historically, should be increased.

— Management will be able to leverage public access applications that provide access to extensive vendor networks and their products in horizontal or vertical marketplaces.

— Moving processes online should result in labor cost savings.

Market forces are promoting marketplaces that encompass several contiguous verticals, rather than a single vertical focus of products or services. In hybrid market-place exchanges, managers of individual verticals will continue to need a great deal of domain expertise. However, they will also be able to cross-pollinate and leverage the capabilities of other market-places to benefit each one of their industries individually. This will promote eProcurement offerings that are moving toward one-stop shopping, while providing vertical-specific services.

In the medium-term we anticipate that eBusiness ecosystems will emerge as the next wave of eProcurement solutions. These interconnected worlds will allow organisations (employees, suppliers and customers) to transact via a single point for commerce and information, creating a global web of digital markets and corporate exchanges.

Global Distribution Network

From traditional road-side hotel signs to modem computer networks, consumers have always based much of their travel decisions on information. The travel business -and every other portion of its distribution chain, including suppliers, intermediaries and customers -is experiencing intense competition for the dissemination of information (including price and availability). The entire $200 billion travel and leisure industry worldwide has a stake in how travel information is distributed, and stands to gain or lose much in the emerging distribution model.

As technologies continue to evolve, competing for the consumer purchase will increasingly take place in the virtual arena as players battle for "electronic shelf space." As a result, the competition for electronic shelf space on the Global Distribution Network (GDN) is of critical importance in an industry where perception is reality and service is increasingly defined by technological advancements, rather than human interaction solely. The GDN is transforming the dynamics of the distribution environment-typified by the unrelenting clamor for the best position in the electronic market. As a result, travel and leisure industry companies must reevaluate their strategic positions in the distribution chain.

Direct access to customers, the bread and butter of the existing value chain, remains at the forefront in terms of strategic direction. Indeed, the electronic shelf space can be defined as the "real estate found on the computer screen. Almost all hospitality transactions taking place today, except for small country inns in Europe or the United States, employ some form of computer terminal where hotel availability is checked and reserved.

For call center reservation agents, travel agents and individuals booking through the Internet, the physical screen, which displays GDN information, is the location of the virtual shelf space. Controlling electronic shelf space—and the number of "eyes" that view GDN information through one specific portal into this virtual inventory is of utmost importance to the world's leading hospitality and travel companies.

Global Distribution System (GDN)

At its inception, the Global Distribution System (GDS) represented a closed, dedicated connection of terminals displaying travel information about airlines, hotels, car rentals, cruises and other travel products. Used almost exclusively by travel agents, the GDS created a distribution chain that was relatively linear, allowing each chain player to collect a portion of the transaction. Today, however, the GDS has been reduced to just one component of a much larger ecosystem of networked travel information with advances in communication and software.

It is this larger structure—the Global Distribution Network or GDN-that is dramatically affecting how business is done in the hospitality and travel industries. This emerging distribution model might be more closely described as a multi-dimensional flow of information and transactions—with any intermediary in the channel able to distribute travel information and complete a transaction directly with the customer.

Unlike many consumer products, which are displayed on physical store shelves, some degree of computerised inventory and distribution system is essential to display hospitality product information. Just as each supermarket aisle displays individual, physical items, specific domains and locations in electronic commerce house hospitality information. GDS providers, such as Galileo, Apollo, Worldspan or Sabre, often represent these domains.

Increasingly, however, Internet-based travel companies, on-line access providers and other virtual communities appeal directly to consumers and travel agents, thereby circumventing the traditional GDS. As a result, hospitality and travel suppliers must develop comprehensive channel management strategies to maximise yield for each existing channel and new component. In addition to the existing GDS, online access providers, Internet service providers, virtual communities, emerging intermediaries and direct connectivity among different suppliers must all be considered and evaluated separately as part of a channel management strategy.

Electronic Shelf Space

Traditionally, the electronic shelf space was found in two places: either the travel agent's desktop or at the reservation center of individual suppliers (accessed by consumers via the telephone). The airline or hotel supplier was connected to travel agents through the GDS, which created a straightforward variable cost structure to sell travel products. Although designed for the airlines, the GDS's widespread distribution (currently 40,000 terminals worldwide) attracted other hospitality and travel companies to list their inventory.

Since their information is displayed in a similar format to airlines, hotel, car rental and tour wholesaler products are compromised on the GDS because of limited description and display of information, as well as the inability to sell inventory directly from a central reservation system. The inventory is essentially on consignment to the GDS at a pre-determined price, regardless of market fluctuations after the product allotment was made available. The end-consumer, travel agents and suppliers had two forms of communication the GDS terminal or the telephone.

With the evolution of the Internet, however, the shelf space has grown exponentially and become much more complex. In fact, the electronic shelf space is now quite crowded. Many suppliers (hotel, airline, and car rental companies) tour and travel companies, virtual agents and travel agents maintain web sites and conduct business over the Internet. In addition, some web sites offer various levels of travel information and advice, most of which are linked to one or more of the above booking engines.

Channel Management

Channel management for hospitality and travel companies requires more than simply understanding the value chain and managing the players. Hospitality companies will need to develop business measurements that effectively represent digital commerce, determining the health and profitability of each available channel. Effective information auditing and analysis will become standard in each organisation's sales strategy. Tools such as decision-support systems, data warehousing, and On Line Analytical Process (OLAP) systems will be required to respond to the market dynamics of each channel and its customers.

Completing a customer-initiated transaction includes product maintenance. information inquiries, inventory access and technical infrastructure to support these distribution developments. Indeed, Jupiter Communications, a new media research firm helping companies make business decisions about consumer interactivity, believes the largest opportunity for sellers of complex travel products—such as cruises and rooms at resorts - lies in integrating the online channel into existing sales channels to reduce the sales cost. Integrated sales channels will help travel companies qualify customers online, reducing the number of calls to close sales of higher-priced products off-line.

Technology by itself does not provide the solution, however. The creative integration and use of today's emerging channel network provides the potential for successful distribution management. Each travel supplier is required to carefully thread each customer through the most effective channel. Requiring excellent coordination between any intermediary and supplier, the functional success to the customer is measured by accurate and timely information on an electronic shelf that owns the greatest amount of computer screen real estate.

Hospitality and Travel Players

The hospitality and travel players battling for electronic shelf space can be found in three major categories Suppliers, Intermediaries and Customers. Suppliers contract to provide travel information in various channels for a fee. Channel providers pass the travel information onto the customers and seek to motivate certain customers to use their channel with incentive fees. Individual customers might receive incentive fees from the channel provider and commissions from the supplier.

Each player has its own set of challenges for management. Past business strategies do not apply to the GDN. The virtual communities of the GDN have unique business requirements as they are created with players clustering around themes or connected interests. It is these virtual communities that form the "neighborhoods" where customers tend to congregate. Each cluster is focused on information services, products, customer demographics or new business models that take advantage of the new technologies.

Tactics for building the customer relationship include developing virtual communities from strategic alliances between companies such as America Online and Preview Travel. Strategic alliances such as these are creating more attractive virtual communities by providing an appealing product and services. Customer participation is a very important characteristic in virtual communities because it is the one factor that differentiates this model from other markets.

The behaviour of travel agents on the GDS and customers who are currently buying products and services online clearly indicate that companies can increase the volume of transactions in their digital channels. Companies have the opportunity to increase service levels, provide personalised interaction that builds customer loyalty, and provide new services that have been previously unavailable. Companies that understand the GDN will benefit from these valuable resources.

Travel Supply Arena

Players in the travel supply arena include airlines, hotels, rental car companies and tour and travel wholesalers involved in the provision of air, lodging, tours, car hire and destination services for travellers. The challenge for suppliers will be to manage and control the multiple entities that make up their GDN. Companies that participate in virtual communities must be willing to relinquish portions of inventory control and capacity management. Existing yield management techniques will need to be adapted to allow companies to effectively participate in the GDN.

The rate at which distribution channels are changing is alarming. Suppliers will be challenged to determine the level of integrating the GDN into their organisation. Suppliers in general seem to lack a vision of where the GDN market is going and the role technology is playing in determining the future of the travel industry. In addition, the high cost of distribution is now causing many suppliers to reevaluate current distribution strategies.

Intermediaries

These companies include internet providers, Telephony/ Call Centers (Worldwide toll-free numbers automatic call detection systems, GDS marketing media solutions) and Universal Switch Providers. These switches are communications devices that translate, convert and exchange information between hotel systems (CRS's or PMS's and airline GDS's). Universal switches assist the travel supplier by providing suppliers with "one-stop shopping" for equal access to the assorted GDS providers. The hotel supplier currently is the only beneficiary of switch providers.

Numerous opportunities exist for additional universal switch players for hotel as well as other travel suppliers. Suppliers that go direct to the customer represent an obvious threat to intermediaries. Any player in the value chain can pirate a customer from an intermediary in the GDN. Channel providers have the potential to leverage strong existing virtual communities by adding new products and services to the value chain immediately. Travel suppliers that create direct links to customers will be able to chip away from intermediaries.

Customers

Entities with direct access to customers include travel agents, online travel agents, Internet/online service providers, corporate travel departments, company representatives that coordinate travel for employees, and individual travellers or agents acting on behalf of the consuming traveller. Clearly, the role of travel agents has evolved rapidly as they seek to remain competitive given the growth of the electronic shelf space. In simple terms, travel agents no longer serve as order-takers holding the monopoly on GDS access. In the new distribution model, travel agents become knowledge brokers, serving as travel consultants who add validity and credibility to the information.

Hospitality companies will benefit as they conduct feasibility studies investigating how to build presence on an electronic shelf space and determining which distribution channel to select. In the virtual community, linking multiple suppliers, destinations, and products is effortless when compared to a physical one-stop shopping center. Customers are eager to access all information with as few clicks as possible, whether they are travel agents, corporate travel planners or end consumers. And finding which customers are most profitable becomes an additional task of effective channel management. Virtual communities are much like physical ones, with large differences in interests, incomes and demographics.

Mobile Executive in a Global Economy

With the evolution of a global marketplace, however, attitudes toward assignments out of the home country, as well as provision for compensation and benefits, have shifted significantly in the hospitality and leisure industries. For the truly mobile executive, the strongest development route may now be through a variety of international assignments with that individual bearing some of the "cost" of the assignment in return for stronger career development prospects. To retain and motivate executives accepting assignments outside the home country, it is important to remunerate them accordingly.

Nevertheless, payroll and related costs often account for as much as 45-60 percent of hotel expenses, and it is crucial that the costs of such transfers be controlled. In addition, new and more flexible approaches to compensating those executives accepting overseas assignments are evolving to match the needs of companies and employees in a global economy.

The traditional approach to compensating executives transferred from home countries in the past involved a central assumption—executives will be reluctant to take on an overseas assignment, and therefore the process should be as painless as possible. The so-called *Balance Sheet* approach has broadly aimed to maintain the individual's home country spending power in the new host country. Once an individual with the requisite expertise was identified and the family/personal issues were resolved, the company developed a package to ensure the individual was not adversely affected financially by the assignment. The individual's basic pay was augmented with additional entitlements or allowances to cover the following:

— Cost of living (COLA);

— Expatriate premium;

— Housing;
— Education (for individuals with families);
— Home leave;
— Professional tax advice; Tax protection/tax equalisation.

When possible and practical, an individual generally continues to pay contributions to social security, pension schemes, and life and medical coverage in the home country. As a result, if the individual is transferred to a country or area with a high cost of living or a more costly taxation regime, providing a remuneration package can prove to be very expensive. The Balance Sheet approach is relatively easy to understand, reduces suspicion that the executive is being disadvantaged, and by virtue of the fact that the executive is well remunerated, aids mobility. In addition, however, it can be:

— Expensive for the employer;
— Focused on the net benefit to the employee rather than driving down costs for the employer;
— Probably outdated as employers move to a global approach.

Tax Equalisation and Protection

To ensure that the employee is not financially worse off, tax equalisation and protection schemes are often adopted. In a tax equalisation scheme, a hypothetical amount of home country tax is calculated on the usual elements of compensation (i.e. excluding extra amounts received as a result of the assignment). The employer withholds the hypothetical tax while paying the actual tax liabilities to the employee's home and host countries. There is often an extra cost associated with this payment of an employee's tax liability by the employer, as this generally creates further taxable income, and therefore there is a tax on tax or 'gross up' effect.

At the end of the year the final hypothetical tax liability is calculated and any under-,or over-payment of hypothetical tax is paid by, or reimbursed to, the employee. Consequently, the executive who has been transferred is no better or worse off than before the assignment. Any benefits arising from tax planning within these schemes are benefits to the company. With a tax protection scheme the employee is responsible for actual tax and social security liabilities in both the home and overseas countries. These liabilities are then compared to the liability that would have risen had the assignment not taken place and any additional tax costs are reimbursed on a grossed-up basis. As a result, the employee cannot be worse off, but may receive a tax windfall if the actual costs are lower than they would have been in the employee's home country.

Net Pay Schemes

Net pay schemes are also a common feature of such assignments. Hypothetical tax and social security is calculated dependent upon an individual's salary, family size and other factors. The individual's pay, net of this amount, is guaranteed. The employer then assumes responsibility for all actual tax liabilities which are paid on a grossed-up basis. Usually net pay is also augmented by allowances for the individual. An advantage of this method is that no year-end reconciliation is needed as the net pay is guaranteed beforehand.

Pre-Assignment Planning

Tax protection or equalisation in a high tax environment can be very expensive for the employer. Planning an assignment, therefore, is crucial to reducing the associated costs as far as possible. Much can be done to limit the impact of taxes, including:

— Taking advantage of potential tax treaty exemptions. This may require consideration of the number of days spent in the foreign country, and who should be the employer or who should bear the employee's costs.

— Qualifying as a non-resident in years of arrival and departure, and consequently being taxed at a lower rate or not taxed at all. Timing here can be crucial.

— Maximising advantages of graduated tax rates.

— Delivering related allowances as cost effectively as possible. For example, home country social security costs may be saved if a portion of the allowance is paid by the employer as a direct payment to a third party for services such as housing. This is in contrast to providing a cash allowance to the employee, which would be subject to social security contributions.

— Using opportunities such as separate employment arrangements and special premiums for work outside the foreign country.

Pension consideration

Pensions are another important area for consideration to ensure that pension contributions/coverage are not disrupted. For a short-term assignment an employee generally would continue contributing to his or her home country scheme. However, this may not necessarily be the most tax efficient planning for an individual on a longer term assignment, who possibly may not return to the home country. A solution adopted in the hotel sector involves establishing a worldwide unapproved plan to prevent employees accumulating limited pension entitlements in several locations. In this case, the benefits of maintaining one single fund outweigh the reduced tax efficiency.

Estate tax issues

Inheritance or estate taxes are frequently overlooked when planning an assignment. Generally employers will pay for professional advice in resolving complications with overseas and home country taxes as a result of an employee's death during his or her time away from the home country.

Globalisation

Globalisation puts considerable pressure on human resource personnel to re-evaluate the traditional methods of providing for executive assignments and to develop innovative new packages suitable for the globalised economy. This represents an increased challenge to human resource personnel during a time when head counts for support functions are under scrutiny.

In addition to the traditional expatriate moving to a specific assignment country and back, typically with a specific technical skill, there is a new breed of mobile executive who has no home country, but rather moves from location to location with career progression a primary motivator. For the latter, a single rigid policy covering different types of employees will be ineffective, and a more flexible, global policy is required.

Localisation

Expatriate assignments also are becoming longer-term because of changes in the business environment. Such expatriates may have adapted to the host country way of life, and as the employer has made the up-front investment in transferring the individual overseas, a solution needs to be identified to phase the individual onto local terms and conditions. The key to a successful transition will be the presentation of the reasons and methodology of the transition policy to the individual in a way which is easily understood and accepted.

Destination Web Strategy in Hospitality

A Destination Web Strategy means leveraging the popularity of your destination to your own advantage by making your hotel or cluster of hotels the "hero" of the destination, and in the same time turning your hotel website into a valuable destination resource for your online customers and increasing its value and relevance for the search engines. This strategy is one of the most effective means to market a local property or a cluster of properties within a particular destination. It allows the hotel to leverage the richness of the destination and shape the local attributes of its environment with creative marketing initiatives that appeal to its online customer base.

The strategy is also an imperative for hoteliers to highlight the property within the context of local resources, because local government sponsored initiatives to promote the richness of the destination, which includes your hotel, are quickly diminishing. Hotel planning is destination sensitive. When searching for accommodations on the Internet, consumers usually use keywords based on the name of the destination +hotel, e.g. "Boston Hotel".

An estimated 85% of Internet users rely on search engines to locate information on the Web (e.g. Yahoo, Google, MSN, AltaVista, etc). Independent hotels, branded hotels, hotel management companies and lodging companies must all rely on search engine referrals. So by having a robust Destination Web Strategy, the search engines will be able to find additional value in your website, catalogue and index the website more effectively, associate it more specifically with various local attractions, lifestyle attributes and aspects of the destination, and drive more business to the property.

Hoteliers able to leverage the popularity of their destination, matched with a well-defined hotel product mix, can capture more online market share and boost conversion rates. The key ingredient is by promoting the many facets of the hotel and cluster of hotels and its relationship to the destination. This approach allows for creative flexibility by making the hotel always the center of attention, the "hero of the destination."

Types of Destination Web Initiatives

A Destination Web Strategy can take many forms and shapes based on the particular destination or business environment. Here are the most common types of initiatives:

— *Destination Section or Page*: An optimised destination section or page within the hotel website of a single hotel property or a corporate website that represents a cluster of hotels in a given destination.

— *Destination 1-Pager*: A stand-alone fully optimised one-page website representing a cluster of hotels within a destination.

— *Destination Website (single property)*: A stand-alone website encompassing destination attributes matched with attributes of the hotel. (e.g. eco travellers, gamblers, spa enthusiasts)

— *Destination Web Portal*: A stand-alone multi-page fully optimised website representing a cluster of hotels with local area content, pages targeting different audiences (e.g. business travellers, leisure travellers, etc).

Some hotel companies, guided by Internet-savvy consultancies, have already begun employing Destination Web Strategies to counter the disastrous effects of merchant model discounts and better market their product and local destination attributes. Whether the hotelier has one hotel or cluster of hotels, a Destination Web Strategy enables the hotelier to offer a rich, deep, destination focused website with the creative flexibility of appealing to a variety of patrons. These may be: conventions, meetings, groups, business and leisure travellers, lifestyle activity seekers, family, weddings, honeymoons, recreation, etc.

A Destination Web Strategy is an exercise in evaluating the attributes of the destination, the various aspects of the hotel product, and the relevant lifestyle attributes of your existing and potential customers, and packaging it in a presentable manner for the online consumer. The final product becomes a well defined destination-oriented website that serves as the foundation for creative and innovative online marketing and distribution.

You will now be able throw marketing muscle behind various initiatives in response to societal trends, current events, and general shifts in the market place. This strategy is "natural" for the hospitality vertical as the product, by definition, is destination specific.

This strategy involves conceptualising, developing and optimising the hotel website to achieve two main goals:

— Provide valuable and relevant destination information so that the online travellers and the search engine spiders alike find value on the website beyond the mere hotel product content

— Turn the hotel into the "gravitational center of the destination"

— Developing the Destination Web Strategy is a complex task and requires a combination of Internet, hospitality and destination-specific knowledge and extensive research. Some required steps include:

— Identifying the most popular area attractions
— Identifying the relevant lifestyle categories, attitudes and values of your existing and potential customer base
— Identifying local events that can be exploited to attract guests at the property
— Identifying how local attractions and lifestyle attributes relate to the property
— Identifying patterns of consumer online purchasing habits for the hotel/resort and the particular destination
— Evaluating the most popular target keywords for the destination
— Ranking the keywords according to their popularity and relevance
— Developing credible and relevant copy based on detailed destination research
— Weaving the target keywords throughout the copy
— Developing the "invisible copy": page titles, description tags and meta tags.
— Overhauling your website to add the identified destination, lifestyle and property attributes and position your hotel product as the central point of the destination
— Performing a Destination-Focused Search Engine Strategy

The process for building a destination strategy begins by evaluating typology, attributes, and resources in the local environment. Identify your type of destination. Next identify all the external attributes within your area. The destination may offer outdoor recreation services, an extensive transportation infrastructure, seasonal events and attractions, major business districts, conference centers and much more. After the destination is analysed, begin evaluating and introducing the hotel product and the lifestyle attributes of your customer base into the mix.

The product mix may include: wedding facility, conference room, meetings and reception area, and concierge services, while the customer profile may include business travellers, senior travellers, and even families with pets. The lifestyle attributes are more complex. Identifying the attitudes and values of a person or group, and sometimes of people that you have never seen or heard from (e.g. potential customers) is inevitably more difficult.

Different characteristics of the property or destination can appeal to different customer segments. For example, to the business traveller, choosing a hotel may be influenced by the availability of a function room, high-speed Internet access or proximity to an area corporation, while a leisure traveller may find the same hotel a great location for local area attractions; same hotel, same destination, different purpose.

Benefits

The Destination Web Strategy allows for a highly informative, content rich website that encourages site references for increased link popularity that boosts search engine positioning. The creative flexibility of this strategy captures key customer segments and shapes the property with a variety of new, varied and exciting insights for the online consumer. It attracts new customers seeking choice, particular in lifestyle categories, plan meetings or weddings, or provide close proximity to a convention center. This strategy can be configured to appeal to any audience where there is relevance to the local destination.

Since the Internet provides unprecedented flexibility to shape locally relevant content at relatively low cost, a Destination Web Strategy becomes a source of "permanent innovation" for the hotelier. Exploiting the existing popularity of the destination and leveraging the appeal of the local market to various customer segments boosts direct-to-consumer distribution over the Internet at a very reasonable cost. The need is very real as the environment is increasingly more competitive and traditional marketing channels and even government supported efforts are diminishing.

2

Human Capital in Hospitality Industry

The hospitality industry has traditionally focused much of its attention on the assets it best understands—real property and the capital that finances it. And yet what will distinguish the most successful companies of the next century will be the effective management of people, information and customer relationships—the industry's intangible assets.

Today's industry leaders are therefore challenged to develop the tools which will measure, manage and influence these intangible assets as they contribute increasingly to the value of business enterprises. In dealing with this challenge, our industry's leadership must consider an array of issues confronting the people side of our business—the methods for learning more about our customers—and how we recruit, train and develop our employees.

Human Capital Resources

Human resources (HR) as an important feature of long-term planning and nearly three-quarters felt their human resource practices, policies and procedures were aligned with their overall business strategy. As to the impact of technology, opinion was evenly split as to whether it will reduce the number of general staff required in the future, although there were some important differences regionally. In Asia / Pacific, close to two-thirds felt that technology would have this impact.

The role of HR management is not always clear in today's hospitality companies. Clearly the human resource function of the future will have a more bottom-line business orientation than it has had in the past. For this transition to be effective, however, a greater alignment of human capital management with the core business strategy will be required, coupled with more sophisticated measurements of performance. While the human resource function gets redefined within the organisation, its component parts are on offer without. Increasingly popular as a tool for more effective business management, outsourcing appears destined to make in-roads into the HR function, part of a larger trend toward increased use of specialised vendors and other partners. In the future, we can expect to see more HR functions outsourced with one-third of respondents seeing training and benefits administration as outsource candidates for their organisations in the future.

Recruiting people to the hospitality industry is unfortunately only one of today's human capital challenges. Employee retention appears to be just as big a headache and it may get worse before it gets better. To counter this, approximately two-thirds of respondents plan an array of strategies, including the increased use of incentive pay, more job enrichment programmes, improved working conditions, improved screening tools and increases in benefits.

Once recruited, a number of strategies are used to reduce employee turnover—some effective, others less so. Improving the work environment, sharing information and increasing employee involvement in decision making are some of the leading choices. This suggests, however, that the hospitality industry may continue to find itself at a disadvantage when competing for qualified employees with better-paying industries. In looking at what contributes the most to employee turnover, there does not appear to be an overwhelmingly strong view in favor of any one factor. In order of significance, they were compensation, hours of work, opportunity for employment in other industries, benefits, work conditions, internal opportunity for growth and finally the image of the industry itself.

The relevance of hospitality education is an important issue for the industry as technology, finance and marketing become big drivers for success. Customer service as a vital educational issue—clearly a wellplaced priority that positions the customer at the center of the universe. An impressive majority of respondents also identified marketing as an important educational focus - a reflection of the growing competitiveness of the industry and of its increasing orientation to the customer.

Training and Development

As hospitality organisations plan for the training and development of their employees in the future, they will evidently need to work more on their planning process—the current view is fairly negative. While just over two-thirds of respondents agreed that their training plan was 'effective', only 18 percent could "strongly agree" with such a statement. And one-third of respondents either took no position or viewed their plan as ineffective responses which suggest plenty of room for improvement.

As to training methods—"on the job" appears to be the dominant theme, although this approach should diminish somewhat in the future. Some of the more popular development programmes include multi-skilling, cross-training and career succession - and there are clear plans to significantly expand their use in the future. There also appears to be widespread use of employee participation programmes—close to two-thirds of respondents cite the use of suggestion schemes—a fairly traditional approach, while a surprisingly high 46 percent indicate job enrichment programmes and 43 percent so-called "quality circles".

Hospitality organisations also use a variety of methods to identify workplace issues and for the most part intend to significantly increase their use in the future. In US, employee surveys, currently used by 70 percent of respondents, are planned for an increase in the future. And while 68 percent of respondents acknowledge the use of suggestion boxes—the "employee" equivalent of the guest comment card—use of these passive instruments is expected to decline in the future.

Productivity Challenge

As human capital becomes more expensive to recruit, train and develop, increasing attention is being devoted to those factors that affect productivity. Empowerment, education, training, recognition programmes and technology will all play different roles in this area in the future. The area with greatest prospective impact on productivity appears not surprisingly, to be training. Three out of four respondents held that empowerment, education, career advancement, incentive and recognition programmes would also have strong impacts on productivity in the future. Somewhat less impactful, was the role of technology.

Relationship between Employee and Customer Satisfaction

In view of the evident relationship between employee and

customer satisfaction, to rank the different approaches to improving the former. Employee recognition programmes, the opportunity for career advancement and exposure to training followed in order of impact. Improving performance is desirable but it also needs to be measured.

In developing an integrated measurement system, the first step is to develop an accurate accounting of employee satisfaction. And to this end, a variety of methods are reportedly used. Employee surveys are destined for much greater usage in the future. And finally, upward evaluations now used by 18 percent are expected to more than double in use in the future.

Hospitality organisations around the globe appear to have set their priorities and will hopefully pursue these with the same vigor that they have historically applied in other areas of this complex capital and people intensive business. And for those that do, they will be in a far better position to compete in a world market space where human relationships and information will be valued far more highly than the physical assets that have been so central a part of the industry's makeup and psyche in the past.

3

TRAINING IN HOSPITALITY INDUSTRY

Travel and tourism represents a broad range of related industries. The growth of these industries has opened up many new job opportunities for graduates in areas such as:

— hotels

— restaurants

— retailing

— transportation

— travel agencies

— tour companies

— tourist attractions

— leisure, recreation and sport

— cultural industries

It is interesting to realise that in 1997 travel and tourism provides 10.5% of the total world employment, with up to 25% of all employment, in some areas, such as the Caribbean. It has been estimated that, by 2007, more than 100 million people world-wide will be employed in this sector. Because of this, tourism is now seen to be of importance to most countries of the world.

During this time, the nature of tourism has developed in scope and direction, away from traditional activities, such as the sunshine sand and sea holidays to a wide range of new activities such as cultural tourism, adventure tourism, sports and leisure activities and eco-tourism.

Given the potential for interesting and rewarding careers in these industries many young people are looking for suitable courses which will help prepare them for careers in management within the tourism and hospitality industries. When looking at courses in hospitality and tourism, there can seem to be a bewildering variety of course titles covering the main employment areas of travel, tourism, hotels and restaurants.

Strategic Model of Training

The hospitality industry is now considering putting much effort on education, and of the element to be paid attention is training and development. Rapid changing in environment must be dealt with 'freedom' of creativity, new approaches to staff, dealing with new technology conveying learning into their life at work, flexibility in organisation model, etc have become part of daily activities. All these issues are really now the driving forces for the hospitality industry to 'tap in' into the current environment. The question is how the whole 'perplexing' issues can be answered in today's business life.

The hospitality industry ought to rely on model of strategic business management to accelerate the sensitivity of growing expectations from customers. The model below attempts to accommodate the variety of issues in today's environment as part of the strategic model. The hospitality industry must realise that designing a model of the strategic management ought to be looking at the wide range of components that might be affecting its performance.

One of the main thing should be addressed is the dynamic environment. All aspects of factors beyond the industry have put in place before proceeding to the plan. Identifying the variety of environment can be valuable for both the company and its clients. No longer 'gambling' or 'intuitive' or 'personal feelings' recommendation to establish the business objectives. One thing should be done is compiling significant information of existing market and trying to break them down into scale of priorities.

One of the difficulties facing the hospitality industry these days is hiring the skilled person(s) to synthesise relevant information. The critical point here is the hospitality industry must be able to accommodate its current resources and be persistent about where we want to go. A lot of experts argue that a strategic management model can only be applied to anticipate the changing environment.

Unfortunately, this is not right. What managers should do is developing the model and 'engineering' the environment to fit with the proposed model. One possible method is to create a market that attracts customers to come, and ensure they will come back again. Price and quality could have been used as the tools to create new opportunities. The model above might be used to put some ideas to fix the old paradigm of 'anticipating' and 'adjusting' model and move to a 'dynamic' model that can be flexible in current and future environment.

By (always) related back to your vision and strategic objectives, the hospitality industry has to catch up with future environment. The problem within the hospitality industry is having a lack of vision, and the industry has only long-term strategic plans. What happens with the

environment is it changes rapidly. Therefor
hospitality industry must make and develop its strat
model to speed up its role of current and future
environment. This means that the hospitality industry ought to focus primarily upon the needs of all employees be reoriented to changing conditions.

The human aspects should be given more attention in today's environment. The model above depicted that understanding and underlying the importance of the strategic business objectives in line with corporate vision should be transformed into 'transferable manner' that employees might able to follow them up. Thus, it certainly requires management's support (i. e. motivation, reinforcement, reward and recognition). The central focus on this model is the hospitality industry must come up with strategies to achieve goals.

One possible strategy is to provide training and development that will lead to learning. Encouraging learning has become one of an international theme within the hospitality industry. There have been a lot of discussions in this matter whether an organisation should provide a specific training for a specific job or we offer a training package leading to multiskilling employees. This is "an old song in the new rhythms".

The issue is not just be able to improve skills, but mastered in specific skills instead. The main concern in the hospitality industry that customers demand professionalism on the jobs. If you are able to have different skills for different jobs, that's excellent. But, don't get too excited not being able to provide an outstanding service. The principle for the training process therefore getting new personnel and current staff to be able to play a role to the success of the organisation and then how the services or products of the organisation can contribute to society.

The model indicates that the first step to be taken is induction programmes that are familiarising new employees to the organisation, their job, and the work unit. During induction programmes, the hospitality industry tend to explain in details about the philosophy, culture, ways doing things, etc. This is quite right in one side to ensure that new employees are able to identify their current internal environment. However, this could be downgrading employees' expectation that may have different approaches about the existing atmosphere.

Instead of giving employees a bulk of big manuals to them, it would be better off for employees to adapt and be motivated that your contribution is really significant for our goals. One way to attain this is through socialisation that encourages employees to unite with current employees. Socialisation is the process through which new employees acquire the knowledge, skills, and attitudes that make them successful and to be integrated to the organisation and work department.

Be ensure that the training programmes can and must encourage participants to learn, and managers have to motivate them to ensure that they will apply the new acquired skills in the worksite and learning transfer should be prioritised among managers. Conducting evaluation would be the possible tool to find out whether training has been transferred or not is.

Evaluation may be the least area to be considered and developed. Having 'smile sheets' is insufficient to render judgment about the effectiveness of your training activities, but it must involve the whole components (i. e. trainees' reaction, learning issues, behaviour and results) to find out how effective the programmes are. When the evaluation is completed, we are able to expect that the outcomes are positive and rewarding, both for those responsible for the programmes and for managers who will make decisions derived from their evaluation training programmes.

The basic issue in the hospitality industry that a certain model must be developed to endeavor to lead in the future market. The hospitality industry a picture of how necessary every step should be considered to execute the training programmes. Working on wrong assumptions may lead to design inappropriate training programmes that could create 'an undesired outcomes'. The current issues occurred in the workforce and attempt to 'tap in' into the model.

The model into the current issues is the hospitality industry will be in favor position to compete in a world environment that in line with companies' vision and strategic objectives by designing the appropriate training programmes. More importantly, human relationships, information and willing to change will be seen as very imperative to attain desired outcomes. The model chosen attempts to accommodate the topical themes in the hospitality industry.

Training in Serving Customers

Training is about skills, knowledge and attitudes. Training is nothing more than providing you with the basic ability to provide uniformly high standards of service (how). An individual can demonstrate his or her ability (skills) to perform, then this individual does not require any more training. If someone possesses 'an adequate' skill, thus training is necessary to perform tasks 'according to standards'.

To explore here is 'something' beyond the training programmes for persons who have had enough experience in the field. This may have been hidden for quiet long time. Again, in the hospitality industry, managers tend to seek someone who has a basic skill to perform (how well), and then from that basis, a new employee will be assigned to undertake further training to 'polish' with work standards (how). Thus, it appears that your past experience is 'only' working during recruitment and selection process.

Training programme is provided in line with the work standards. Most of the training managers have their own agenda to supply the industry with 'qualified staff' and this has to be done to achieve companies' vision and strategic objectives. However, there is one missing point here that the training programmes offered may far than staff's expectations. Experienced staff does not want any 'basic' skills anymore, but using his or her past experience to jump up to the next level, therefore, they require management development programmes. Managers may argue that we 'expect' you to serve our guests according to the manuals and should follow literally.

Everything has run smoothly and beautifully and there were not any mistakes. At the end of the day, managers will evaluate and give you a positive feedback. However, it was not the way it works at this hotel. The hotel expects you differently. It is only a matter of the 'right way' to service guests. The word 'expect' will sound explicitly. It can be seen that what happens to staff depends not just upon "how well" you serve, but also upon "how" you serve customers. "How well" you serve is related to individuals' skills, whereas "how" you serve customers is a matter of work procedures.

Having had work experience is the good one and this may be useful to support your career progress. But, once again, if you have failed to execute the hotel work standards, it seemed unlikely for every staff to be promoted. Originally, training programmes in the hospitality industry purpose:

— to support staff with basic skills required to perform tasks,
— to provide additional training (if it is required) to reduce the performance discrepancies, or to support for a new position,

— to supply employees to be able to carry the company's banner,
— to provide for staff with new acquired knowledge to achieve customers' expectation,
— to offer staff with 'appropriate' attitudes, and certain knowledge,
— lastly, managers expect staff to work uniformly high standards

Training Accountability

Training is generally acknowledged as an important 'vehicle' for the hospitality industry. There have been a lot of facts, reviews and manuscripts to support this. Besides, generally known that training is also seen as an investment rather than just 'a regular programme' activity. Indeed, lots of researchers have acknowledged that the traditional view of training entails the following three components that can be useful to render the effectiveness of training programmes.

— A methodical assessment of training needs analysis to ensure that a training programme addresses issues and problems within the hospitality industry. A thorough needs analysis is used to determine where in the organisation training is needed, which employees require training, and what knowledge and or skills are required.
— Applying an appropriate training tools/methods to deliver content based on training needs analysis. The training methods depend upon the programme's objectives. Methods can be on the job training or off the job instruction. And each method is best utilized under particular conditions determined by the desired outcomes.

— A wide-ranging evaluation of the programme applying numerous different evaluation criteria and strategies to ascertain whether the desired outcomes have been achieved.

However, the problem appears to be narrowed on training specific features per se and it also seems that these components exclude such consideration of factors outside the training boundaries that could influence the effectiveness of any training effort. This outside factors could be individual and work environment that may also associate with training effectiveness.

Therefore, training effectiveness, which is arguably, may not be able to stand firm with the instructional design and or contextual factors alone, but it may be caused by some 'unidentified factors' that tend to be 'left out' in every single discussion. Therefore, it is very interesting to explore what these 'unidentified factors' are.

Many questions have been arisen in educational literatures or empirical evidence that managers should ask how much money we spent on training in relation to employees' perceptions of the value of training. Although, it may be useful to know whether perceptions about training are in line with companies' financial commitments to this activity, it seems that the question has gone to the wrong address.

The issue is not 'how much', or 'what employees' think', or 'what methods', but the issue is of what makes training effective. Nevertheless, such an approach suggests that if desired results are not achieved with a considerable level of training expenditure, perceptions, or delivery issues, management will search for a reason for the failure and probably focusing on to the one of the three components above or could be all of them. Thus, such a failure may in fact have nothing to do with the training itself, because 'unidentified factors' may affect training effectiveness. The next thing is trying to find out the factors outside the training boundaries that appear to influence training effectiveness.

Characteristics of Individuals

— Individual's ability to learn and acquire new knowledge and skills can have a direct influence on training preparation and performance. Some of the factors that individual should have is his or her ability to construct and evaluate problematical information. If trainees possess these, thus learning would be comparatively quick and efficient. Individuals' ability can be assessed throughout the selection process and to make selection decisions, managers must know about the skills, knowledge and attitudes required to perform the essential tasks and duties.

— An individual's attitude toward work may also affect his or her willingness to apply the newly acquired knowledge and skills on the job after training has been accomplished. Such individuals' commitment should also be considered to ensure his or her desire to achieve good performance. Indeed, if individuals possess a high degree of commitment to their jobs, it is very likely they will regard training as valuable and easy to transfer their new 'capital' back on the job.

— Individuals' willingness may lead to increase their motivation. In addition, those who are motivated to go to training are more likely to learn and use their newly acquired knowledge and skills to the workplace. Now the issue is how to enhance motivation. It is managers' job to boost their motivation and to understand employees' values and needs. To find out which motivation—either external motivation or internal motivation or can be both—, managers must constantly examine and work together with their employees.

Working Boundaries

— Working atmosphere may have a considerable impact on someone's preparation for and transfer of training. Hospitality managers must be concerned with factors such as individuals awareness about the work situation and systems as they influence learning and performance.

— Social association may also play a major element of the work environment that can influence training effectiveness. Organisation's social norms and values that support learning can have a positive impact on an individual's willingness to attend and learn during training, as well as to transfer learning back to the job. Peers support can also be successful to encourage individuals to use the newly acquired knowledge and skills. 'Buddy' system is very helpful for someone who remains unsure to apply newly gained skills and knowledge.

— Organisational systems such as the appraisal and reward systems. Performance appraisal is used to identify performance discrepancies and this will form the training needs analysis to determine the exact cause of performance gap. Furthermore, if someone can demonstrate a great performance, he or she should be rewarded. And this can be seen through every individual who shows what they have acquired through training.

— Finally, continuing learning may have a major impact on the effectiveness of training. Programs such as mentoring, apprenticeships, traineeships, cadetships, attending professional seminars can too influence the effectiveness of training, especially when these learning opportunities accompaniment what has been gained through training. It should be noted that there is more to training per se than the assessment of needs, methods and proper evaluation. For training to be fully maximised, managers must look beyond the training boundaries and examine the individual and work environment factors that have a significant influence on training effectiveness.

Training Programmes

Most hotels industry has invested their dollars on training. And each of hotel has a number of different ways to evaluate its training programmes and it depends upon the kind of training event, the aims of the training, the diversity of participants. But, still managers have doubt how to conduct evaluation.

Issues such as who should be doing it, what purposes are, how to convince internal/external customers, techniques. The most important aspect needs to be addressed prior to evaluate training programmes is that evaluation should be integrated into strategic business objectives. There have been a lot of recipes of evaluating training programmes in very sophisticated explanations, arguments, charts and so forth but managers remain unclear about the purpose of it.

Firstly, evaluation can supply valuable information on how the programme can be improved or terminated. It also can identify specific difficulties/problems in the organisation, find out which training methods are effective, ascertain the significance of the programme in relations to the participants through improved KSAAE (knowledge, skills, ability, attitude and experience). Indeed, evaluation can too be used to have a promotional agenda. In addition, evaluation is also of concern to achieve cost effectiveness.

Finally, training programmes have to achieve the bottom line of the organisation objectives and this is where performance is linked to the organisational value or results. The "super model" of Kirkpatrick a four-stage evaluation model; reaction, learning, behaviour and results have been refined and revised.

It seems straightforward to write about evaluation and to exhort others to carry out the task, but evaluation itself requires an integrated approach to ensure that training programmes are effective. Evaluation appears to be a complex task, however, it depends upon how managers will do it. And again, every single task that relates to evaluation activities should link to the strategic business objectives. There is no doubt with current theories, models, charts about evaluation and they all seem practicable, but a nagging question is how we value training activities. This can be the reason that evaluating training programmes must relate to the strategic business objectives.

Thinking about training evaluation for the hospitality industry requires a systematic approach to deal with. Indeed, it needs fully supports from managers to make certain that every single dollar spent on training programmes has been achieved. In the hospitality industry, managers (usually) know what KSAAE their employees need to do their jobs, and then training them in those areas and at the end it will produce bottom line results.

Training for front line employees is designed to ensure that they are able to undertake their tasks professionally and in the same manner. A hotel operator, for example, is given a job description before embarking to the actual workplace. Then, he/she will undergo a training programme that corresponds to the job. The job descriptions are:

— pick up the phone after ringing twice,

— say greeting, i. e., good morning hotel A this is Johnston how may I help you?,

— thank you for calling hotel A and your call is connecting. Please hold the line.

— you are on.

Evaluation then seems relatively easy to conduct. If managers / supervisors/subordinates are willing to evaluate their staff, then the first thing they should do is addressing the performance back to the job description. Again, it is only a matter of can and can't do (my previous article) principle. Evaluation must go back to the strategic business objectives that convey mission and vision for the organisation. Another example would be training for front line staff to achieve an 'outstanding' customer service that correspond to the organisation's business objectives.

Training is then provided that supports the organisation's strategic objectives, but is also targeted to employee efforts. Evaluation then can be done through managers, peers or direct supervisors. These triangle sources of information then will make evaluation more valid. More importantly the using of customer service surveys will ensure the organisation that training produce the bottom lines. Herewith some useful tips that may be beneficial for doing evaluation:

— Planning; what do you want to do, what do you want to find out and how you accomplish it?.,

— Sponsorship; managers/supervisors/subordinates should involve in evaluating training activities.,

— Measuring; relates your findings to the strategic business objectives.,

— Data collection method; performance appraisal can be a good source.,

— Your judgments.

Need for Training Analysis

The main problem of textbooks and or journals is predominantly 'crammed with' theoretical framework and lack of empirical evidence. The most effective way conducting TNA and introducing a new integrated model of TNA, however, implementing TNA is left behind.

It is arguable that training and HR professionals always accentuate the significance of linking training to relevant results. Managers know exactly to come to a decision about whether or not to provide training for employees, and what type of training should be offered. Their decision has characteristically been based on the determination of training needs within organisations.

TNA is very critical time for building links between training and results because the first part of decisions are made regarding what training will be given in organisations. The 'traditional' model of TNA which refers to three interrelated phases—needs analysis, execute and re-evaluation is workable in today's environment. The other three sub-aspects such as organisation, task and person analysis may be seen as very important to begin with and managers may have already done it within departments. The current model is okay but need to be supported by empirical evidence to ensure the model works.

Employees have to realise their ability to perform which relates to their daily activities and what sort of training to support his/her performance. The heads of departments have also to evaluate their staffs and find out the appropriate training for their employees if necessary. The most common way to do TNA is distributing a questionnaire. Every head of department has his/her own 'diary' about individuals' performance and the effective way to start of with TNA is checking a 'diary'.

To make more valid, you may also distribute a questionnaire and conduct an interview with the potential staff. Therefore, managers will rely on three sources of information, which are performance appraisal, supervisors/subordinates and employees. From this basis you have sufficient information to design your training modules.

TNA appears to be seen as a snapshot of your future training programmes and the issue is TNA should be updated correspondingly. From this paragraph, distributing a questionnaire, talking to the heads of departments as well as to your staffs, and reviewing performance appraisal will provide sufficient information prior to design your training programmes.

And TNA should also be flexible and adaptable. TNA does not always derive from problems. Training may not always the key to solve problems. For example, if there is a skills problem, therefore training will be the perfect solution. But there are many issues surrounding problems and training would be the last option. Thus, TNA will able to determine whether or not training is necessary. Perhaps more workload would be better option rather than send some one to attend training.

Training is given due to a lot of demands within the hospitality industry. Employees need more training. There are not any problems or performance discrepancies. Staffs need training because they want to learn from his/her peers. Thus, the end goal of TNA is encouraging learning. TNA comes from employees and learning is given the main reason. Here are some common issues/problems of TNA:

— A questionnaire is being regarded as an effective tool to accommodate employees' needs. However, managers tend to give a comprehensive questionnaire that employees might think this is too complicated and this could give you a low response

— Language problem; some of your staffs may come from non-English background. Thus, it would cause language difficulties to fill out the questionnaire.

— Employees have said "so-what". There is not any follow-up afterwards. Training is seen as a regular programme and has nothing to do with the job.

— Be objective; your employees may have illiterate problems. Instructions can be difficult to understand and questions may not correspond to his/her objectives.

— Dealing with casual staffs who do not care about training culture. This might affect your training programmes as well as training results.

— TNA seems to be more informal and employees are able to express their needs to managers.

— TNA may not be seen as an accurate tool to conduct training programmes, but it is seen as a valid starting point of information for managers to develop such a programme.

Quite often in the hospitality industry, training programmes come from the head-office that may not correspond with employees needs. Thus, the purpose of TNA is to modify the 'dropping' programmes that will match with staffs' desired and adjust with local culture. And this truly happens.

Taylored Training Targets

The "core competencies" cover the skills necessary for the continued personal and organisational success in the hospitality industry, including customer service, writing, and meetings skills. To provide the training necessary to put these skills in place. The "managerial competencies" address the leadership and practical skills needed to cultivate an effective and productive managerial force, including sales, leadership and career management.

Communication and team-building are the focus of the "strategic competencies" segment, and the "tactical competencies" cover sales and marketing. Among the current programmes, which can be presented at in-house, off-site, or at regional locations, are:

— Creating a Culture of Customer Service
— ServSafe Food Safety Certification
— Marketing For The Hotel Industry: Understanding The Individual Leisure And Corporate Customer
— Presentation Skills: Staying Calm And Confident Before Two or 2000!
— It's Not Rocket Science!—Boot Camp for New Sales People
— Building A Web Site That Works

Taylored Training's primary resource is a panel of presenters and trainers with extensive and specialised professional experience, giving them unique understanding and insight into all facets of the hospitality industry. Panel expertise may also be drawn upon for conferences, education sessions, meetings and private consultations.

Hotel Bookings through the Internet

Hotel bookings through the Internet, whether on franchise web sites or electronic distribution channels, have risen exponentially. GDS bookings increased in 2003 3. 3% while the Consumer Internet Channel bookings increased by 34. 7%. This has led many hotels and hotel companies to re-allocate sales and marketing resources to managing and manipulating their positioning on the Internet. They are quite correct in doing so—this is a trend that is not only not going away but will continue this kind of growth for at least a few years into the future.

This percentage increase, unfortunately, has not been characteristic of most hotel sales departments and, as a result, the precious marketing resources available to them have, in many cases, been reduced to accommodate the expenditures on Internet channels and web presence. As a result, many hotel sales people have become frustrated and discouraged to the point that they wonder if there is a continuing role for them as this trend continues.

The traditional methods and modes of conducting hotel sales will not produce the results that will alleviate this concern. It is a simple case of "if you keep on doing what you have always done, you will continue to get what you have always gotten." In today's environment, that leads to diminishing returns as travel and meeting planners turn to the Internet more and more to evaluate rate and amenity positioning prior to ever contacting a hotel.

Often, the second step is to visit the web site of a particular property, again prior to contacting the sales department. What can sales departments do to increase productivity, avoid becoming an in-house amenity. Hotels need to include the sales departments in their Internet positioning and web design so that the message and offering is consistent across the customer touch points. In addition, sales departments need to embrace the technology and use the Internet to become more productive and efficient in conducting hotel sales at every step of the sales process.

Target Market Prospecting

In an attempt to locate new markets as existing ones are producing less, the decision is often made to target markets that previously were ignored. This can range from government (all of a sudden per diems don't look so bad from a rate standpoint), SMERF, Affinity groups, etc.

Traditional Sales: Locate existing or dead files for prospects in these target markets then begin contacting them one at a time.

Cyber Sales: Conduct a web search that becomes increasingly specific until a prospect list or database can be located on related web sites.

Market Penetration Strategy

In most cases, it is impossible to ascertain the depth of a market or begin to penetrate it without making contact with a significant number of prospects. How to do this efficiently?

Traditional Sales: They are still contacting the "dead" files. Contacting one individual or organisation with a phone call is very time consuming and not very efficient.

Cyber Sales: Develops an email postcard or an email message with a benefits tease, copies and pastes email addresses into a group on the email address book.

Initial Approach

The name of a prospective organisation and key contact information is available.

Traditional Sales: Pick up the telephone and call them. Upon routing to their voice mail, leave a message with your name, the hotel's name and phone number. Trace it for two weeks, repeat process.

Cyber Sales: Locate the e-mail address on the web site or call the central number, press zero (normally there is still a human available) and ask for the contact's email address. A recent client was absolutely amazed at how willing the receptionist was to give out the email address. This is only a brief glimpse at how hotel sales departments can incorporate the Internet into their every day activities to contact more prospects more efficiently.

Each of the examples above are just the beginning of the techniques that hotel sales departments can use to incorporate the internet into their activities to penetrate target markets, develop new prospects and maintain relationships. People are now used to initiating and building business relationships through email, instant messaging, etc. Once we have "touched" them enough times electronically, it is then possible to make a telephone appointment to build on the relationship.

A telephone appointment is more efficient than leaving voice mails. The message here is that hotel sales departments can use the Internet in many ways to become more productive and efficient. As the growth in use of the Internet channels exhibits, our prospect find us in new ways—we need to find them in the ways that they locate us. Yes, there is still a role for hotel sales departments to play if they become more creative efficient in conducting sales activity. It is exciting to be in a position to re-define the hotel sales process—use your imagination.

4

Skills in the Hospitality Industry

In the context of hospitality, skills issue is informed by wider, generic debate about changing employment and vocational education within both developed and developing economies. Hospitality work exhibits diversity in both horizontal and vertical terms. In a horizontal sense, it includes a very wide range of jobs, the extent depending upon the definition of the sector that is employed. The traditional research focus on hospitality work concentrates on areas that provide, primarily, food and beverage and, to a lesser extent, accommodation.

Research into wider areas of hospitality work, particularly those that have emerged with the expansion of services and functions in the area (front desk, leisure, entertainment, reservations call centres) is much more poorly served and draws on a limited range of work in these areas. The 'newer' areas include functions and tasks that exhibit considerable crossover with work that falls outside normal definitions of hospitality in food and drink manufacture, office administration, IT systems management and specialist areas of sports and leisure.

Indeed, it is fair to say that although there is long-standing debate as to whether the hospitality industry is 'unique', there is little doubt that there is little that is unique about hospitality skills. Most of the skills that are employed within the sector also have relevance and application in other sectors of the service economy. Those employed in areas where there is considerable skills overlap with hospitality may well see themselves in terms of their generic skills area rather than as part of the hospitality labour market and some of these skills have been subject to separate assessment in a manner that has value and crossover implications for the hospitality sector.

The characteristics and the organisation of the hospitality industry are subject to on-going re-structuring and evolutionary change. There are major labour market and skills implications of such change as businesses re-shape the range of services they offer or respond to fashion and trend imperatives in the consumer marketplace. Vertical diversity in hospitality work is represented by a more traditional classification that ranges from unskilled through semi-skilled and skilled to supervisory and management. This 'traditional' perspective of work and, therefore, skills in hospitality is partly described by Riley, in terms that suggest that the proportionate breakdown of the workforce in hospitality is as follows:

Managerial - 6%

Supervisory - 8%

Craft (skilled) - 22%

Operative (semi-skilled and unskilled) - 64%

This simplification masks major business organisational diversity in hospitality, reflecting the size, location and ownership of hospitality businesses. The actual job and skills content of work in hospitality is predicated upon these factors so that common job titles (for example, restaurant manager, sous chef) almost certainly mask a very different range of responsibilities, tasks and skills within jobs in different establishments.

Riley is useful in his application of the weak-strong internal labour market model to illustrate the relationship that his workforce structure has to a number of externalities including educational requirements, points of entry into the workforce, workplace pay differentials and level of trade union membership. This analysis has important ramifications for the status of hospitality work and the perceived attractiveness of the sector both for employment and educational/training opportunity. Some of the researchers summarise a list of the characteristics of hospitality work that tend to confirm Riley's weak internal labour market attribution:

— Tendency to low wages, except where skills shortages act to counter this.

— Prevalence of unsocial hours and family unfriendly shift patterns.

— Rare incidence of equal opportunities policies and male domination of higher level, better paid work.

— Poor or non-existent career structures.

— Informal recruitment practices.

— Failure to adopt formalised 'good' or 'best' practice models of human resource management and development.

— Lack of any significant trade union presence.

— High levels of labour turnover.

— Difficulties in recruitment and retention.

The skills profile of hospitality, in turn, is influenced by the labour market that is available to it, both in direct terms and via educational and training establishments. The weak internal labour market characteristics in themselves impose downward pressures on the skills expectations that employers have of their staff and this, in turn, influences the nature and level of training which the educational system delivers. There is an evident cycle of down-skilling, not so much in response to the actual demands of hospitality work or of consumer expectations of what it can deliver, but as a result of the perceptions of potential employees and the expectations that employers have of them.

Hospitality work is widely characterised in both the popular press and in research-based academic sources as dominated by a low skills profile or, as brutally and, probably, unfairly put it, 'uneducated, unmotivated, untrained, unskilled and unproductive.' However, Burns questions the basis for categorising hospitality employment into 'skilled' and 'unskilled' categories, arguing the postmodernist case that this separation is something of a social construct that is rooted in, firstly, manpower planning paradigms for the manufacturing sector and, secondly, in the traditional power of trade unions to control entry into the workplace through lengthy apprenticeships.

Burns bases this argument on a useful consideration of the definition of skills in hospitality, noting that: ...the different sectors that comprise tourism-as-industry take different approaches to their human resources, and that some of these differences...are due to whether or not the employees have a history of being 'organised' (either in terms of trade unions or staff associations with formalised communication procedures).

This strong internal labour market analysis leads Burns to argue that skills within 'organised' sectors such as airlines and hotel companies with clearly defined staff relationship structures are recognised and valued. By contrast, catering and fast food 'operate within a business culture where labour is seen in terms of costs which must be kept at the lowest possible level' and where skills, therefore, are not valued or developed. Burns' definition of hospitality skills also seeks to go beyond the purely technical capabilities that those using 'unskilled' or 'low skills' descriptors assume.

He draws upon the oft used dramaturgical analogy for the service workplace to argue that 'Working in such an environment requires more than an ability to operate a cash register; emotional demands are made of employees to constantly be in a positive, joyful and even playful mood. An ability to cope with such demands must be recognised as a "skill" par excellence.' New employees in hospitality 'Must be trained to be loyal, flexible, tolerant, amiable and responsible...at every successful tourism establishment, it is the employees that stand out...Technology cannot substitute for welcoming employees.'

Burns' emphasis on 'emotional demands' as an additional dimension of hospitality skills. Work in both fast food and traditional areas of service work areas demands considerable emotional elements in addition to any overt technical skills. Furthermore, Burns rightly argues that the low skills perspective of hospitality is contextspecific and is drawn from a western-centric view of hospitality work and skills generally. He cites the inappropriateness of these assumptions when applied to environments such as the Solomon Islands, Sri Lanka and the Cook Islands.

In the developing world, such assumptions cannot be made as employees join hospitality businesses without western acculturation, without knowledge of the implements and ingredients of western cookery, for example. Learning at a technical level, therefore, is considerably more demanding than it might be in western communities. Social and inter-personal skills also demand considerably more by way of prior learning, whether this pertains to language skills or wider cultural communications.

The current hospitality labour market in the Republic of Ireland illustrates this situation where service standards are under challenge as the industry recruits staff from a wide range of former eastern block countries. A government-sponsored response has been to organise special training programmes of three months duration for new workers from Poland and Russia. The low skills argument also tends to neglect the opportunities that hospitality provides for the relatively easy access to the use of entrepreneurial and management skills.

Weak internal labour market characteristics mean that it is readily feasible for those with limited specific hospitality or business training to enter the industry at ownership or senior management levels, especially in the independent sector. The aim of many who enter the sector is to eventually start up their own business. Others may choose to do so after careers in different areas of employment or enterprise, perhaps for 'lifestyle' reasons. What they have in common is the desire to build upon a skills base in hospitality that may be relatively limited in order to utilise wider enterprise and business skills within the sector. On this basis, the initial or base skills that are used to describe hospitality work do not provide a complete basis for describing the nature of work in the sector.

It is clear that there is no ready resolution to this 'low skills debate'. Reich's occupational typology identifies three discreet categories:

— High-level symbolic manipulators or analysts.

— A dwindling group of those engaged in routine production.

— A group providing interpersonal services - waiters, hotel receptionists among others.

Within this classification, it is clear that skills which are most highly valued in society fall within the first category.

Hospitality work, on the face of it, falls, in part, into the second category (chefs) and predominantly into the growing third category, a grouping that does not readily accommodate the consequences of the arguments of Burns or those relating to emotional labour.

De-skilling

De-skilling is an inevitable consequence of growing standardisation or routinisation across the service sector. There is evidence to support this process in hospitality and tourism in the form of a growing fast food sector; within budget accommodation; and through the growth of no-frills airlines. The growth of these sectors all point to a simplification of tasks in the workplace, aided in part by technology substitution but also by changes in consumer demands and expectations. It is also arguable that these sectors have grown in response to new consumer demand as opposed to displacement of demand for traditional services.

Therefore, while their growth may have had the global effect of 'dumbing down' average skills levels in hospitality and tourism, it is difficult to argue that they have eliminated demand for higher order skills within other sectors of the industry. Some of the research analysis shows:

— Traditional skills and functional boundaries breaking down in many occupations, leading not to functional fragmentation, but to multi-skilling in more integrated tasks.

— The effect on skills not easy to predict, due to different management strategies on task reorganisation.

— Relatively little de-skilling, disproportionately concentrated on lower skill and craftlevel jobs where barriers to cross-trade re-skilling had reduced the potential for integration.

— Much inter-occupational hybridisation of skills at all occupational levels and in manufacturing and service sectors, combined with both up-skilling and de-skilling.

— Demand for higher-level occupations stimulated by the effect of structural trends and labour supply on employers' interpretation of skill needs.

Hospitality is moving towards increasingly multi-skilled models of training and work has been aired since the early 1980s. The focus of this argument has been targeted towards meeting employer needs, particularly in smaller businesses where the notion of flexible rotation between different hotel departments in a way to suit the demand cycle is presented as a logical business solution.

In reality, such work represents multi-tasking because the level and nature of the work in question (food service, bar service, portering, housekeeping) offers little by way of enhancing the actual skills of employees other than extending the operational context within which they are exercised. One of the specialist educational programme represents the accumulation of complementary but not progressive skills in various hotel departments.

The issue of multi-skilling or multi-tasking should be seen in the context of organisational change within hospitality and the manner in which organisations are separating core employees in whom significant training and skills development is invested and those at the periphery for whom such enhancement is not common. It is argued that developing skills across a range of functional areas enhances the likelihood of acceptance within the core although evidence for this is not readily available. Creating the opportunity to develop a wider range of skills within the workplace is frequently included within models of job enrichment.

Multi-skilling or multi-tasking across departments, as generally practiced within the hospitality sector, does not offer much to employees that can be described as 'enriching'. Of probably greater value to employees is the breakdown of job demarcation within hospitality departments, such as the virtual elimination of the traditional partie system within kitchens and the merging of front office functions (cashier, reception, concierge) in many hotels.

Technical or Generic Skills

Skills shortages in hospitality are increasingly seen in terms of generic rather than specific technical competencies. Studies of employer expectations of graduates note demand for communications, people management and problem solving. It is, of course, an issue that informs a debate across the service sector - see for example, Tesco as well as within the wider economy with their development of core or key skills. Qualifications and Curriculum Authority (QCA) identifies key skills as:

— Communications.

— Application of number.

— Information Technology.

— Working with others.

— Improving own learning and performance.

These key skills represent capabilities that have, traditionally, been integrated as 'normal' expectations within hospitality curricula at operational and management levels and a specific focus on the development of these skills, outside main curriculum delivery objectives, may be questionable in the context of this sector.

However, Hospitality Training Foundation (HtF) continue to report employer demands for improved generic skills as a priority. These skills include communications, showing initiative, delivering customer service and demonstrating a willingness to learn. Recommendations to tackle the generic skills gap include:

— Building generic skills development into full-time education programmes.

— Funding for training providers to deliver key skills and develop appropriate aptitudes and attitudes within young people.

— Ensuring providers are developed to be able to deliver key skills.

— Recruitment practices need to encompass generic skills requirements.

HtF's Delphi study of skills requirements in hospitality also reports that the skills gaps, as seen by the hospitality industry, focus on what can be styled the generic agenda - communications, problem solving and customer service in addition to job specific skills.

Empirical evidence from a study of front office work and skills requirements across a number of European countries shows clearly that this focus operates in practice. Hotels in all quality categories in seven European countries recruit on the basis of generic employability rather than specific skills and experience. Even five star hotels 'accept the reality of the marketplace and are willing to recruit staff without Front Office experience provided they have good general education and a willingness to learn.' The same report also notes that:

A key evolving change in Front Office work is the integration of technical and interpersonal skills in all aspects of work. This is the result of a growing emphasis on the latter while technology has developed as a support for the delivery of service rather than as an objective in itself. In a technical sense, technology will continue to reduce the skills demands of Front Office work as systems become more user friendly and share their basic operating features with widely used office and domestic computer software.

The weakening of traditional workplace hierarchies in front office, with a decline in the position of junior or assistant receptionist so that given 'the virtual elimination of traditional, routine office-related tasks such as basic typing, filing and photocopying, it is, in any case, difficult to distinguish between the job content' of various levels of work within the area. In the absence of experienced, qualified staff, many hotels will increasingly look to generic, non-technical competencies (communication, problem solving, customer service and IT) in recruiting new personnel and build in extended on-the-job-training within the induction phase'.

In addition to these generic skills considerations, some of the studies suggests that aesthetic criteria also feature increasingly prominently in the recruitment of front line staff for hospitality work. HtF's skills and employment forecasts raise an interesting paradox in the hospitality skills debate. Employers, as has been demonstrated, place value on generic skills such as the willingness to learn and the ability to be flexible and adaptive. At the same time, initiative is also a valued skill and one found to be lacking in the industry. HtF raise two important questions:

— Are employers being unrealistic in their expectations? People who are good at following instructions may not be able to show much initiative.

— Are employers recruiting the 'right' people? If, when recruiting, employers focus on people they feel are good at following instructions, they may find later that they cannot expect them to show much initiative.

These questions are of particular relevance in the context of trends towards and advocacy for greater empowerment in learning and work. The concept of empowerment is presented in the hospitality management literature as a human resource strategy with relatively widespread application.

EDUCATION/TRAINING PROCESS IN HOSPITALITY

The development of skills to meet the needs of various stakeholders in hospitality is frequently seen as a partnership between the industry and the educational/ training providers, with each playing a complementary role. The extent of their respective involvement depends upon the objectives and level of training as well as upon the system in which such training is located.

Guerra and Peroni note a relatively homogeneous hospitality industry but point to considerable diversity within the educational and training systems that operate alongside the industry, reflecting differences in national vocational education systems as well as diversity in the status and focus of tourism and hospitality at a national or regional level. This diversity is clearly reflected in the structure of hospitality skills programmes in different countries. Within the German apprenticeship system, apprentices spend the majority of their training time in the workplace with a short, normally eight-week release period to college within any one-year.

Higher level education and training for hospitality and tourism generally maintains a clear commitment to the development of skills designed to complement more generic educational and business development objectives. In the hospitality context, some of the researchers considers the changing role of practical, vocational education within hospitality degree programmes and note considerable retrenchment but not elimination of this process.

Within hospitality, a key skills issue that is bound up in the traditions of the sector is the significance of food and beverage skills development as a necessary stepping stone towards the application of general management skills within hotels. A study of the careers of hotel managers confirms the widely held perception that food and beverage experience remains the single dominant career characteristic of successful general managers although the revenue contribution of this area is relatively less important than that of accommodation. Few successful general managers have significant training or experience in rooms, accounting and marketing functions prior to their entry into general management. This suggests a continuing focus on traditional food and beverage skills development within the educational process despite the stated expectations of employers.

The importance of the debate that addresses the fit between hospitality industry 'needs' and the programmes provided within the vocational education and training system. This is a complex issue and there is relatively little evidence to suggest that 'industry needs' are represented by a single perspective. Indeed, given the diversity within the industry, it is unlikely that unanimity could ever be achieved with respect to the training and education that is required. Educational providers should tailor their skills development provision to meet the needs of a targeted segment of the industry rather than attempting to be 'all things to all hospitality businesses'. It is also an argument against the notion of a core or common curriculum for tourism or hospitality education.

Traditional models of education and training for hospitality place considerable responsibility for skills development and the consolidation of learning on vocational work experience or internship. Researchers describes the process as one that benefits all three stakeholders involved and is valued: By education, because the trainees were getting an opportunity to learn more about the structure of the industry in a more formalised way; by the tourism industry because trainees proved to be a useful source of inexpensive skilled or semi-skilled labour on a regular basis; and by the trainees themselves because the work experience has resolved a vicious circle into a career opportunity. The value of working experience as part of a platform for skills development towards job finding and career development is widely accepted.

5

Cultural Dimensions of Hospitality

In a service encounter a tourist and a waiter engage in the culture of service and the waiter performs emotional labour in addition to performing technical skills. The actors in the service encounter bring to the interaction their own ethnic identities and engage in cross—cultural communication. To ensure the provision of appropriate hospitality service human resource development must take account of the cultural dimensions of hospitality.

Abundance of cultural and natural attractions they have lured tourists from a variety of culturally diverse generating regions. At that time tourism in Indonesia was virtually non-existent. At the same time the Government of Singapore had eliminated its tourism programme on the grounds that tourism was "frivolous" and "too vague" to be of use to the economy.

The pursuit of inbound tourism as a prominent component of national economic life has, in recent years, not been confined to the foundation members of ASEAN. While those states have continued to expand their frontiers of tourism to provide new attractions for tourists, other Southeast Asian states have begun to pursue economic diversification through international tourism, For various reasons these states, until recently, had not been prime destinations for travellers.

According to the World Travel and Tourism Council the Asia Pacific region's tourism industry is still in its infancy and therefore the full impact of tourism is yet to be realised. Whilst tourism growth in the region provides cause for optimism, it has already created labour supply problems for employers.

There will be increased pressure on these countries to provide the skilled labour needed for quality service. Although current economic conditions in Japan are affecting outbound tourism in that country resulting in more Japanese taking their holiday at home, nevertheless Ilakim believes that, so far as outbound Japanese tourism is concerned, the majority of the jobs catering for their needs will be in the customer contact area. It is here that there will be a need for host countries in the Asia-Pacific region to have customer contact people who can communicate effectively and sensitively with the Japanese.

The competitive edge of an economy is not found in its commodities or low wage labour, but in the contribution of a rising quality labour which can provide high levels of service. Thus the notion of quality service will play a crucial role in the economic contribution of tourism and hospitality to the region. As quality service is possibly the foremost determinant of success in the tourism and hospitality business it is important that the focus be placed on improving service.

If more tourists are to be attracted to the region, it is imperative that the strategy is not put in jeopardy by the lack of quality service. It is, however, one thing to identify the need for quality service, but it is entirely another matter as to how such a service might be supplied. The tourism and hospitality industry in the Asia Pacific region has an image problem which results in government, employers and prospective employees all sharing reservations about the nature of the industry itself. For example, the industry is perceived by potential employees as being dominated by expatriate staff in its key managerial and professional positions thereby offering limited career opportunities to the domestic work force.

It is also perceived as offering low status employment for young adults or marginally skilled workers, a situation which may well lead governments to conclude that it is a minor player in the economic life of a country. Its poor image as an employer is reinforced when students undertake work experience during their industry placements. Tourism and hospitality are so negatively affected by their hotel placement that they choose not to enter the industry because they feel they are being used as cheap labour or as fodder for the operational needs of the hotel.

This lack of service to the student appears to emanate from areas of the hotel industry that should know better, namely the Human Resource (HR) people and departmental heads who apparently believe students are incapable of thinking through a problem with which they are confronted. Given such an image, the issue of the industry being able to recruit talent and expertise to its ranks is a very serious matter indeed.

If talented potential employees believe there is little or no opportunity for recognition, advancement and reward, then the question must be asked as to the calibre of employees ultimately recruited to serve the ever expanding tourist market. Fortunately there are bright spots in this disturbing picture when it comes to the recruitment and placement of people in the industry

Lessons may be learned from the approach of a Taiwanese hotel to the recruitment of talented employees. This involved the use of a variety of marketing approaches involving direct mail, flyers, window displays, magazine articles, hotel tours, school presentations, exhibition booths, and an internship programme. Through these means potential employees have been attracted to a career in the hotel industry. There is also a 'Casual Club' to recruit part-time workers, giving these people a sense of belonging to the hotel. Whilst the marketing of recruitment seems reasonably well handled among employers of the region, more attention appears to be needed in the area of effective selection and placement of employees.

There is no doubt that the region has been experiencing labour shortages particularly in the areas of managerial, professional, skilled and semi-skilled labour, and to a lesser extent of unskilled labour. Whilst cross border labour movement is in part offsetting labour shortages. labour movements are increasingly likely to pose problems for some parts of the region as countries struggle to ensure that jobs are available for their own nationals who have become unemployed by the current economic crisis.

The current emphasis on management training to the detriment of skilled, semi-skilled and unskilled jobs raises the question as to just how well non-managerial employees in hospitality are being prepared to provide customer service There is also the question of how well the existing service is being delivered and whether visitors leave with a favourable impression of a destination as well as a desire to visit the destination again.

Culture of Service in Hospitality

In relation to hospitality provision the culture of service refers to the values and meanings which underlie hospitality and give it its essential quality. Essential to hospitality are the reception and entertainment of guests who are to be provided with psychological and physiological comfort and security. Hospitality includes both tangible and intangible services. When a service encounter takes place between a tourist and a waiter, both are engaging in the culture of service.

In performing the required technical skill for serving the food and drink, the waiter provides the tangible service. The social interaction between the waiter and the tourist is the intangible service and contributes to the tourist's total experience. According to Powers, the social interaction requires genuine warmth and friendliness and necessitates empathy.

Service Provision

Service provision is a situational social process provided at an appropriate level and catering for individual needs. This kind of labour in which emotion plays a key role is referred to as emotional labour. It as exploitation of emotion. It as labour that 'calls for the coordination of mind and feeling' for the purpose of producing 'the proper state of mind in others'. The establishment of a contrived emotional relationship through emotional labour is 'difficult and demanding, under-recognised and relatively under-rewarded'. The relationship is also an unequal relationship between the recipient of the service who is dependent on the service job for employment.

Culture of Identity

The actors in the service encounter bring to the interaction their own ethnic/national identities. Using the language of the computer age we can discribe cultural identity. This kind of culture as 'the collective programming of the mind which distinguishes the members of one group or category of people from another'. The programming involves the establishment within the person of 'patterns of thinking, feeling, and potential acting' which Hofstede calls 'the software of the mind'.

Culture of this kind is learned from the various groups within which a person interacts during the course of his or her lifetime. The family, for example, plays a major role in the cultural development of an individual. According to Hofstede, much of this cultural development is acquired during early childhood 'when a person is most susceptible to learning and assimilating'.

Cultural differences are demonstrated in a variety of ways. In some societies, for example, great respect is accorded to age to a degree not evident in other societies. Ideas about personal space vary from culture to culture. In some cultures, making eye contact during verbal communication is unacceptable; in other cultures eye contact is important as a sign of openness. These various examples of cultural difference are generalisations. Besides belonging to cultural groups people are also unique personalities. Uniqueness does not, however, diminish the importance of culture. Uniqueness does know bounds; these bounds are set by the cultural groups with which individuals identify.

While language differences are likely to be the most obvious component of cross- cultural service encounters, there are other aspects of Hofstede's 'software of the mind' that need to be taken into account. For example, what 'collective programming of the mind' has taken place to influence the attitude of a young man or woman towards the desirability of being a waiter in a restaurant? Anecdotal evidence from Southeast Asian tourism and hospitality students in Australia suggests that such a job is not considered desirable for its own sake.

Instead it is seen as a way to make money for immediate living expenses and, in the long term, as a springboard for a managerial position. In some cases there is reluctance to learn what are considered to be the more menial hospitality skills. If the job is not highly regarded within the cultural group, how will this affect the waiter's enthusiasm for and performance in the job? There is also the likelihood that the 'collective programming of the mind' has included animosity between cultural groups. Will this animosity affect the service encounters between members of those groups?

The major issues associated with the cultural dimensions of service. The service received in a host country is often judged by the tourist's own cultural standards. For example, the Asia Pacific region is host to approximately 10 million Japanese tourists each year. There is a great chance that visitors to the region will find customer contact people either unaware of or unable to respond to their clients' needs.

Tourists in foreign lands are likely to be in search of cultural knowledge and experience. Whilst this knowledge and experience is formally provided by tour operators and guides they employ, informally hospitality service providers such as waiters and receptionists may, through conversations with guests, serve as another source of cultural knowledge.

Anecdotal evidence from tourists who have visited Bali, for example, indicates service encounters in restaurants during which young Balinese waiters, anxious to practise their English, engage with guests in the exchange of knowledge about their respective cultures. In some cases friendships are formed, correspondence is exchanged and contacts are renewed on repeat visits to Bali. In the anthropological literature, the waiter performing this role is described as a culture broker. 'Culture brokers are found in all cross-cultural situations... amongst taxi drivers, tourist guides, tourist police, security guards, hotel workers and market vendors. They act as mediators between tourists and the resident population'.

In this capacity they play an important part in enhancing the tourists' experience of a destination.

Culture of the Organisation

The way that management mobilises combinations of values, language, rituals and myths' in order to unlock 'the commitment and enthusiasm of employees'. The outcome of a positive organisational culture in terms of the employees 'sense of belonging to the organisation' combined with 'a sense of enrichment in the job, and confidence in management'. Critical concept of organisational culture and its links with commitment, arguably it may be possible to draw from their descriptions dimensions of organisational culture appropriate to large and small enterprises which provide hospitality services.

If the idea is accepted that the service encounter has the potential to provide intangible as well as tangible benefits, it would seem to follow that management should have in place the appropriate 'combinations of values, language, rituals and myths' to encourage 'the commitment and enthusiasm of the employees' in enhancing the tourist's total experience.

When service is examined within the context of hospitality organisations, it can calls affective and continuance commitment responses from employees. Positive feelings of identification and involvement with their organisation develop an emotional attachment to it. This results in employees wanting to maintain their tenure, relate positively to their customers and provide the customer with quality service. Service as involving intimacy with the customer as well as a concern in providing a quality service for the consumer. Terms continuance commitment where employees, through longevity of service and past promotions, feel trapped in their employment. If these employees left their organisation it would be at great financial and personal cost to themselves and their plateaued careers.

Continuance commitment people were found to relate less positively, and in some cases, even negatively to their customers as well as doing no more than was necessary to maintain their membership of the organisation. Those organisations that succeed in winning emotional commitment from their employees and engage in career development are likely to be better service providers than those that have employees who feel trapped with nowhere to go. For people serving time in their organisation their own needs may become more important than serving the customer.

Human Resource Development

Human Resource Development has improved performance as its ultimate goal in order to enhance the competitiveness and efficiency of an organisation. The term HRD is made up of three core components:

— training to improve the performance of employees in their current job,

— education to develop the whole person for future roles and responsibilities which as yet remain unknown,

— and development which prepares people for their responsibilities in the short to medium term of their career.

As tourism and hospitality is one of the largest and fastest growing industries in the world, it has, in the view of the WTTC, a need to address increased and improved tourism education in the region. This step is necessary in order to accommodate and adapt to ever increasing pressure on tourism and hospitality resources in the region. HRD is one of the most widely used terms in Asia-Pacific gatherings because it is seen as central to the competitive edge of the economy of a nation.

The key HRD stakeholders in any country are its HRD providers, supporters and users in terms of government, employers, and educational institutions. Tourists also are indirectly stakeholders in that they receive the benefit or otherwise of the outcomes and effectiveness of HRD initiatives. Governments will not become involved in HRD initiatives unless they believe tourism can make a positive contribution to their economy.

As tourism employs 1 in 9 of the work force of the world, and it is predicted by 2005 to contribute some 2. 0 trillion dollars from travel and gross output in the Asia Pacific region, it would seem good economic sense for government to support well constructed arguments for quality improvements in the industry.

Technical skills are not the only component of hospitality service encounters, in any HRD strategy they obviously cannot be ignored. Ideally the development of a programme for skills development should be a joint project for industry and vocational education which together bring to the task an understanding of the requirements of industry and an appreciation of the pedagogical factors involved in providing training for skills development. The refinement of competency—based modules and train the trainer programmes in recent years means that standardised training can take place in vocational education institutions and in the workplace through on - the -job training.

Within the domain of skills development, there i5 the opportunity to empower employees by engaging them in a process of commitment to quality service When skills are applied within a Quality framework, these can be used to achieve satisfying service outcomes. If employees are engaged actively in continually improving their service processes to meet the needs of their customers, hospitality service provision will be the beneficiary. For example, through their direct contact with customers in a bar, hospitality staff may become aware that long queues form no matter how expertly they perform their skills.

Because of their first-hand knowledge of the situation, bar staff, if consulted, may recommend a change to the work process such as a series of minibars within the establishment to reduce time pressures on staff and satisfy their customers. In this instance both the customer and staff experience satisfying outcomes.

Developing a Culture of Service

Competency-based modules for skills development cannot guarantee the inculcation of the values which underpin the culture of service. Customer relations modules, through role play methodology, may attempt to develop behaviours which are supposed to indicate a commitment to the emotional content of service but such behaviours are mere surface acting and may lack the ring of sincerity.

While there are good reasons for the 'stereotyped forms of address' and the programmed presentation of service in fast food restaurants, it is unlikely that many customers take the performance seriously. Crang likens the performance of emotional labour to a theatrical event directed by management. While surface acting training is one means of preparing people for their roles as service-givers, Crang also draws attention to staff training 'in a deeper Stanislavskian level of performance', that is, deep acting which, if Hochschild's view is accepted, can have a psychologically damaging effect upon the performers because they lose touch with their true feelings.

If acting, either surface or deep, is inappropriate, how then can a truly genuine culture of service be developed. At the level of management in a hospitality enterprise there must be a genuine appreciation of the values underlying the culture of service and an understanding of what constitutes a positive total experience for guests. This genuine appreciation is reflected in the manner in which staff are recruited with attention being given to the recruitment of people with personality characteristics suitable for empathetic service provision. It is also reflected in the culture of the organisation which creates 'a sense of enrichment in the job'.

Besides providing suitable role models who exemplify authentic concern for the customer. These criteria for appropriate management have implications for the education of managers who, besides needing studies in business and management, would have a greater understanding of the importance of the psychosocial dimensions of hospitality provision through in-depth study of relevant social sciences such as sociology and psychology. This understanding would encompass both the psychosocial dimensions of the tourist experience as well as the need for protection of the psychological well-being of the service workers from the deleterious effects of emotional labour.

Cross-cultural Dimension

The hospitality worker is likely to work in a multicultural environment. Besides the cross-cultural encounters front of house, there are also back of house encounters which have their own cultural dimension. While globalisation may result in superficial cultural homogenisation, the strength of traditional values and attitudes developed over many centuries should not be underestimated.

The Chinese chef, for example, is the end result of a long established Confucian tradition which is not shared by the Irish waiter. Each is the product of a particular cultural programming. How should hospitality workers be prepared for interactions with a multicultural clientele and a multicultural workforce? Within current hospitality education and training programmes one may find components relating to cross-cultural communication. The danger with short courses such as these is that they will highlight the apparently exotic aspects of a culture and thus encourage stereotyping and ridicule.

Cross-cultural understanding may be best achieved by a long-term systematic development of cultural knowledge beginning in elementary school. Any human resource development strategy in terms of the cultural dimensions of service ought to have its roots in the elementary education of a nation. Such an education should highlight humanity's shared experiences as well as cultural diversity and should span all the years of one's education.

Status of Hospitality

Service work in hospitality has low status as an occupation. At the same time the customer contact aspect of hospitality, it has been argued, plays an important role in the total tourist experience. It therefore seems imperative to take steps to raise the status of the occupation. One way in which an attempt can be made to achieve this goal is through educational provision for careers in hospitality. While considerable attention has been given to management training, more attention needs to be given to the integration of operational training into educational programmes at degree level.

There are, no doubt, several ways in which this can be achieved. For example, a degree may be constructed by building a one or two-year programme at university on to a two-year programme at vocational college. Alternatively, a three or four-year degree programme may be taken concurrently with a hospitality programme at a vocational college. The latter approach has the advantage of introducing students to the culture of academic reflection from the beginning of tertiary study.

In university circles it is likely that combining vocational and academic study within a degree programme will meet with some disapproval. The old status division between working with the hands and working with the mind has not disappeared. The combination of the two strands within a degree programme, however, has many advantages. It supports an integrated career path for hospitality workers thus helping to overcome the perception that hospitality work is a dead-end job.

It enables students who, through a relatively poor academic performance at school, did not gain entrance to university to prove their capabilities at vocational college and then to have a second chance at a university education. Lifelong learning cannot be constrained by artificial structures in education. In the vocational college component of the degree, assuming that hospitality practitioners are employed as teachers, it puts students in touch with the 'real world' of hospitality.

In Southeast Asia, there is an obvious need to stay abreast of the changing attitudes and interests of the tourism market. Equally important, however, is to keep informed about the attitudes and interests of the host countries, which change as the local people become more financially stable and increasingly aware ot the value of their indigenous culture and natural environment.

Tourism is the single largest revenue producer in the world today, having surpassed the oil industry to claim that distinction. Presently, tourism—related businesses generate an estimated US$2 trillion per year. It is estimated that 15 percent of all jobs throughout the world are directly or indirectly related to tourism. In an effort to get a share of this lucrative market, governments and private developers everywhere are intensifying their efforts to attract visitors.

The most successful will be those who recognise the all—important premise that large-scale resort developments as well as eco-tourism projects must consider the cultural and environmental qualities of the area. Today's international traveler can choose from a wide array of vacation destinations. He won't fly halfway around the world to stay in a hotel facility little different from one he can find at home.

Thus, a distinctive image is crucial to stimulating visitor interest. Many of the areas throughout the world (particularly urban areas) are becoming somewhat homogeneous—if one were to be suddenly dropped in the middle of a typical big city, they might wonder upon the first visual impression, is this Singapore, Sydney, or Seattle?. However, creating a successful destination resort does not require building a fantasyland with a multitude of gimmicks to keep the customers entertained.

True creativity calls for taking the existing natural and cultural attributes of the environment and, with human ingenuity, blending them in such a way that the end result is extraordinarily pleasing. A traveler expects a pleasant change from his customary lifestyle. Producing a destination resort that will give him this change is seldom easy and never accidental. It calls for comprehensive planning, particularly at a time when people are becoming more and more aware of and sensitive to the problems tourism engenders, along with the benefits it brings.

Destination resorts can and should be developed in such a way that they serve as a means for enhancing natural assets and preserving distinctive cultural characteristics. When existing site conditions offer spectacular views or white sand beaches, the problem becomes one of protection and preservation. Without realistic planning, the environment can be damaged to the point where visitors are repelled rather than attracted.

The first step in developing a well—integrated master plan is to evaluate the existing conditions on the proposed development site. Depending on the site, and the available information, this evaluation may require surveys of topography, flora, fauna, soils and geology, water resources, and investigation of cultural resources, socioeconomics, and history as well.

Through this process, unique assets and advantages of the destination are identified, and problem areas are exposed. In this way, valuable natural and cultural resources are not only preserved, but are also utilized and highlighted as amenities of the resort development which can provide the distinctive image which the developer is seeking to achieve. At the same time, features which have been subjected to damage can be de-emphasised, replaced or improved, thus contributing to the overall achievement of quality in the development process.

The master plan is based on a predetermined carrying capacity which reflects optimum ability of the land and natural environment to accommodate man-made development. This necessitates devising ways to accommodate visitors so that they do not destroy, by overcrowding or by overuse, the destination resort's natural amenities and its unique cultural attributes—the very things the visitor wants to experience.

It follow, then, that the tourism master plan must incorporate solutions to pressing environmental and cultural problem. It must function in harmony with nature and in balance with the community. The resort operator who succeeds in reinforcing harmony between society and environmental processes possesses a goose that never stops laying golden eggs.

6

Time-sharing in Hospitality Industry

During the past two years urban timeshare will be a new wave of product in a growing industry. The industry resilient to both economic and lodging downturns. High returns and growth opportunities are forecast for both hotels and independent operators with the industry's credibility and opportunities on the rise as reputable developers join the sector. The latest high-profile entrant promises to aid consumers in evaluating alternative products. It will represent high-quality timeshare properties. The entry of this well known name offers a significant boost for all reputable timeshare businesses.

Even with the strength of the timeshare industry generally, development of urban timeshare projects has lagged. To date, just three urban developments are creating a standard. Urban timeshare would appear to offer distinct advantages to the hospitality industry, but it has yet to be developed to any great degree by companies. A combination of market forces and industry challenges have created short-term hurdles. The long-term prognosis, however, may offer opportunities for developers in a niche sector attracting sophisticated, upscale buyers, who are interested in the urban experience.

One of the major advantages timeshare products offer hospitality groups is the resilience of the sector to economic downturn. Timeshare sales have survived the peaks and troughs characterising the hospitality industry. Timeshare occupancy tends to be more predictable, and the manager of the timeshare units finds it far easier to manage variable costs, particularly labour, than his or her counterpart in the hotel business. The initial economics of urban timeshare look beguiling to a developer.

Consider the economic return if that same project were developed as a timeshare. The "numbers" are clearly tantalising. Two reasons, however, have mitigated against urban timeshare;

— the increased profile and attractiveness of timeshare has coincided with a property boom in the major cities; and

— inability to control marketing costs.

Many developers and botchers alike have considered the viability of timeshare, either on a stand—alone basis or as a mixed-use plan. Property prices have escalated over the past few years, however. At the same time, the return that can be generated from other options (such as serviced apartments) has been sufficiently high to discourage companies from developing an urban timeshare, particularly with the additional risk associated principally with the marketing costs.

Resort timeshares have been successful, in part due to differential pricing and high occupancy rates achieved throughout the year as a result of an attractive climate and a variety of recreational amenities. Likewise, urban timeshare must also be based in locations that can attract visitors throughout the year. In the case of city sites, customers also include corporations. Which may buy blocks of weeks.

These individuals recognised the gap in the market for flexible urban timeshares, which could exploit the "short break" market. A fairly unusual location for European urban timeshares because it does not typically offer the corporate customer potential of cities. Financing issues Once a timeshare site is identified, financing becomes a major issue. particularly for companies that are not well established. There is still widespread institutional anxiety among finance providers for timeshare developments.

Those developers able to obtain development finance generally have an existing relationship with the institution and a track record in timeshare / timeshare sales. The timeshare developer must have a sound business plan with a focus on, and substantiation of, the projected sales volumes.

Those lenders specialising in financing will provide the construction loan principally to secure the provision of consumer financing. Many of the high street banking names are reluctant to provide loans to the industry, although specialist finance providers are beginning to appear. Construction finance for the new players is still very difficult. The Edinburgh Residence was an exception to this rule.

In many respects, marketing and sales costs are the "great unknown" as regards timeshare in general, but more particularly urban timeshare. where there is far less experience on which accurate predictions can he made. The average active project reports marketing and sales costs of 38.5 percent, although 48.2 percent of projects have marketing and sales costs of more than 40 percent.

When a project is confined to a single site, the marketing of an urban timeshare development is a much more difficult problem. The key issue is balancing the need to generate leads and achieve a high conversion rate, whilst minimising marketing costs. The timeshare achieves a 20-25 percent conversion rate with 400-500 families visiting the site a week. On the other hand, uses a third-party company to do its marketing.

However, it also gains a substantial proportion of its customers through in-house affinity relationships in the form of promotional deals. Its total marketing costs amount to only 18 percent of the cost base, which is substantially lower than the industry as a whole. Conversion rates are approximately 30 percent, in contrast to the average market rare of approximately 15 percent.

Timesharing once the proverbial black sheep of the hospitality industry today occupies a coveted position as one of the fastest-growing sectors of resort development and travel globally. Since 1980, timeshare resorts have grown at an annual rate near 20 percent worldwide, while sales volumes now approach $6 billion annually. The industry sailed through the recession earlier in this decade with hardly a ripple. Not surprisingly, it continues to attract keen interest, particularly as the emerging markets of Asia/Pacific report escalating rates of expansion.

Timeshare's reputation clearly has regained some luster since its early years, particularly in mature markets where regulatory frameworks have curbed earlier abuses, including questionable marketing and sales practices. Entry of global hotel brands has heightened credibility, as these companies have seized opportunities to leverage their customer bases and operational skills in a new industry.

And this fall brought the surprise acquisition of Resort Condominiums International, Inc. RCI the global organisation that pioneered timeshare exchange and has been called the backbone of the industry. With this acquisition scheduled for completion by year end. The world's largest hotel franchisor, assumes a dominant position in timesharing in a single stroke.

The exchange organisations are dominated by Resort Condominiums International (RCI) and Interval International, which share a far-flung market, making it possible for members to "swap" an interval at their own resort with comparable properties at member resorts elsewhere in the world.

RCI had already expanded into related services such as an in-house travel agency and Vacation Net, an on-line travel service, as well as partnering with timeshare developers and offering consulting services to them. Now we can expect that HFS will" knit" together RCI customers with its own vast customer base, offering a highly synergistic menu of products and services—including lodging, car rentals through the acquisition of Avis, residential brokerages and numerous other preferred vendor relationships.

By integrating the RCI reservation systems, HFS can further leverage the customer bases of both enterprises and their brands. RCI is no small addition to HFS's growing customer base, generated in part through its 5,200 hotel properties. RCI commands a membership of more than 2 million timeshare owners and 3,000 affiliated vacation resorts- 70 percent of the world vacation ownership market.

All this bodes well for the timeshare industry, which continues to post record growth. Originating in the European Alps in the 1960s, timesharing has long since won a secure place in the travel and leisure industry. More than 3 million households own vacation ownership interests in more than 4,200 properties globally.

The first branded U.S. hospitality company to expand with timesharing in Europe, and this move signals the advance of globalisation. There also are plans afoot for European ventures in the United States, as well as some companies partnering on these projects, including Fairfield and The Global Group. As the number of owners in the United States and the United Kingdom has almost doubled since 1988, there also has been significant growth in owners in the rest of Western Europe, albeit from a much smaller market base, as well as in South Africa, South America, Australia, Mexico and other emerging markets.

Specialised knowledge of how the timeshare product is financed, developed, marketed and operated is somewhat limited in the hospitality industry at large. In the United States, timesharing in its simplest form offers buyers a fee simple interest in a timeshare property, generally conveying a weekly interval each year in an attached, multi-family residential unit.

Timeshare purchasers pay a one-time price for the interval, which the buyer can sell, give or will to a third party similar to any other real estate interest. In Europe, however, the concept of a fee simple purchase does not apply; buyers generally acquire a right to use the property, rather than a direct real estate interest. The timesharing concept thus varies according to laws applicable to both the jurisdiction of the property and its potential buyers.

Typically, a timeshare resort operates in a fashion similar to that of a hotel, with owners and "exchangers" checking in as guests for a one-week period. Owners generally pay annual maintenance fees for the week intervals to cover their pro rata share of ongoing operating expenses. While one-week intervals are most common and provide a standard for exchange purposes, timeshare properties also may offer other combinations, including split-weeks and intervals every other year. The lifetime term of timeshares also varies widely in right-to-use timeshares, most commonly 20, 30, 50 or 60 years.

In recent years, timesharing has experienced a metamorphosis with the emergence of high end properties designed as elaborate resorts. The entry of global hotel and leisure "brands" —including Marriott ,the Disney Vacation Club and Hilton Hotels—has been a major influence. Marriott is the largest hotel company operating timeshare properties in the world, with a total of 25 resorts currently. Initially developing timeshare properties near its Florida theme park, Disney World. Involvement of global brands, however, is primarily a U.S. phenomenon. No major European hotel chains have yet entered this market in any extensive way, and the same currently holds true in Asia/Pacific. This will undoubtedly change as these markets grow.

Meanwhile, the hotel and leisure branded companies have captured a market edge in development of highend timeshare properties, which typically offer major resort amenities. Chain affiliation and brand-name recognition create important synergies, allowing these companies to leverage timeshare sales to a captive customer group. In turn, prospective buyers are assured of a familiar standard of quality and service. The experience gained operating and managing hotels can often be transferred to the successful operation of timeshare resorts.

These resorts tend to operate as part of a dub system, integrated with the hotel or leisure chain and its guest loyalty progrmmes. The global brands also enjoy the financial backing of a secure parent company, alleviating the sales pressure that many companies are subject to in the initial operating years.

In a third category of less expensive properties, many timeshares have been converted from other uses, including hotels, and are generally characterised by one-bedroom and studio products, with limited amenities and secondary locations. These timeshare properties generally have limited on-site facilities and lack a resort "feel." Global branded companies enjoy certain advantages in timesharing, but both smaller and independent companies are also expected to grow rapidly in the near future, particularly with crossover alliances with the hotel industry.

Timeshare Economics

While growth of timesharing has outpaced the hospitality industry during recent years, development of these vacation properties is not for the faint of heart. The cost to market timeshare properties is high, even for properties owned by hotel brands, which have an established identity and loyal customer base. Cost structures currently lack transparency.

Consumers in the past have generally not been fully aware of the costs making up the timeshare price—including the very large percentage devoted to marketing. Established branded hotel and leisure companies have the marketing advantage due to their market identities, and this is likely to have serious ramifications for the remaining timeshare players, who will need to streamline marketing approaches to compete for business. In addition, the resale market for timeshares is extremely thin.

Timeshares often resell at a very significant discount to original cost, plus a commission charge. Specialised organisations continue to enter the market to handle resales on behalf of timeshare owners and consumers. This is still limited, however, as these organisations generally offer fewer options than the timeshare exchange market. Each involves attracting potential timeshare customers by offering short vacation trips, which have been heavily discounted for air and lodging. Some companies report that this approach substantially reduces the overall costs to market timeshares, while generating an additional stream of revenue.

Prospective buyers attracted by these vacation offers tend to be more sophisticated and predisposed to purchase a timeshare unit than people pursued through off premise contact (OPC), the traditional method of marketing in the timeshare industry. To the extent that marketing costs can be controlled, the economics of timeshare projects can be quite profitable if the developer/owner can weather the initial cash-hungry phases of development.

Indeed this has been one of the reasons why branded hotel and leisure companies have been attracted to the market consider a 100-unit timeshare property selling units at $10,000 each based on a 50 interval weeks a year. That unit is theoretically worth $500,000 and the entire property $50 million. Nevertheless, marketing a property takes the lion's share of revenue and those costs are reportedly rising—from 42 percent of revenue in 1990 to 50 percent in 1995. Similarly, building costs as a percentage of total development costs also rose during this same period—climbing from 25 to 30 percent—as timeshare properties compete in a market characterised by rising customer expectations.

And general overhead costs for many companies can also be greater, as timesharing operations become more rigorously managed. All this may add up to thinner profit margins for many companies, making operational efficiencies more critical to safeguard profitability in the long-term. Timeshare developers also make money by providing buyer financing. The interest spread between taking back mortgages on units at interest rates above the developer's capital costs can generate a significant revenue stream. In Europe consumer financing is somewhat more complex due to the number of jurisdictions involved, and varying consumer credit regulations can make the offer of consumer credit cumbersome from an administrative point of view.

All signs suggest that the growth in timesharing will continue unabated for the remainder of this decade. The shape of the industry is in flux, however, with key trends shaping the industry:

Internationalisation: Diverse factors are promoting globalisation of the industry as customers seek to travel outside their own country. One issue to watch—enabling and regulatory legislation for condominiums and timeshares is generally undeveloped in emerging markets, raising fears that the bad name given the U.S. industry in the 1980s may be replicated in areas where the regulatory environment is relatively loose. RCI is actively working to organise trade associations in emerging markets to endorse standards and codes of ethics.

Industry Concentration: The trend toward a concentration of the players in the market is spurred by the branded hotel and leisure companies, which focus not so much on selling a "unit" but marketing a "vacation club" concept, assuring future vacations at a guaranteed price. Under this concept, the chains allow timeshare buyers to purchase points that can be redeemed throughout their hotel and timeshare product base.

As with the existing travel sector, new technology will play a major role, fostering strategic alliances with other industry providers, including airlines, insurance companies and finance companies. Nevertheless, there are likely to be problems associated with selling a longterm product. Chief amongst them is the question of maintaining quality resort properties without subjecting buyers to uncontrolled and unreasonable increases in maintenance fees.

New Timeshare Markets: Urban timeshare properties are generally more costly to develop and operate than resorts, as well as being more complex to manage because they often offer intervals of less than a week. Nevertheless, there are a number of key developments underway. A $70 million project in New York, for example, will create one of the world's largest urban timeshare properties with conversion of the top 10 floors of the Park Central Hotel in midtown Manhattan.

At the same time, the industry continues to look at the possibility of timesharing cruise ships primarily under right-to-use arrangements, to avoid complexities involved with conveying a real estate interest. RCI currently has several houseboats and cruise berths in its system, primarily in the Mediterranean and on the Nile River. Bu the timesharing of cruise ships is still embryonic in development.

Product and Marketing Costs: It is also likely that the future will bring a change in the economics of developing timeshares with a higher proportion of the purchase price actually represented by product cost. This will favor the larger participants with well-known brand identities due to their existing customer loyalty progrmmes and the pulling power of their reputations in the hotel and leisure community.

The timeshare industry thus continues to grow in allure to industry providers, as well as to consumers seeking to benefit from this vacation concept with its global exchange potential. clearly, the industry's negative image has brightened, and consumer acceptance has been achieved on a wide scale.

While the industry dearly faces challenges that will need to be overcome, timesharing will undoubtedly offer important opportunities for expansion for companies in the hospitality industry—both major branded hotel companies and independents. Indeed, it appears likely that the industry can sustain a high growth rate through the decade, particularly as North American and European markets mature, and demand accelerates in the economies of Asia/Pacific.

7

Hospitality Marketing

The hospitality industry is diverse enough for people to work in different areas of interest and still be employed within the hospitality industry. The hospitality industry pays those well who have prepared well. Hospitality management involves the planning, organising, directing and controlling of human and material resources within the lodging, restaurant, travel and tourism, institutional management, recreational management and meeting and convention planning industries. All of these separate yet related segments of the hospitality industry are interrelated to deliver kind and generous services to guests.

The hospitality industry is one of the oldest businesses in history. People have always gone out to eat sometimes and travelled for work or leisure purposes. However, the face of the hospitality industry has changed drastically. The explosion of growth in the hospitality industry demands highly qualified people trained in hospitality management to fill rapidly opening positions. Although African Americans have had a wealth of experience in hospitality, it has not always been positive. In the past African Americans have usually performed in low-level managerial positions in hospitality operations holding positions from the lowest realm in service to now having the realistic opportunity of becoming general managers.

The present hospitality industry is extraordinarily healthy and viable and as a result offers excellent opportunities for African Americans in each of the segments; restaurant management, lodging management, recreational management, travel and tourism, meeting and convention planning and institutional management. Scott announces good news: the opportunities are there. The globalisation of the hospitality industry creates the availability of jobs in virtually every city in the world.

In the growing field of hospitality, it is projected that by the year 2000 an additional two million people will fill new jobs in the industry. According to the U.S. Department of Labor, in the next decade nine out of ten new jobs created will be in the service industry. A degree in hospitality management with a strong emphasis in business administration strengthens your preparation for the industry. In additional to classroom preparation, junior and senior students especially should seek hands-on opportunities such as internships, shadowing experiences and mentoring relationships. Internships are very beneficial to students in that they provide immediate access to the real work world and also are the time for students to make mistakes as they learn.

In planning and preparing for a successful career in hospitality, take advantage of in-house management training programmes and seek mentors which will increase the potential of a steady and timely progression in hospitality. Students obtaining degrees in hospitality are prepared to seek employment in hotels, restaurants, travel and tourism destinations, convention and visitors bureaus, health care facilities, airlines, recreational facilities, and management/contract services, etc.

Successful African Americans in hospitality recognise their role and the importance of mentoring incoming students interested in hospitality management. According to Phillip Cunningham, historically African Americans have not achieved the same level of success in the industry, due to the lack of corporate mentors. It is extremely important to identify people who can help you achieve your goals. Often this means the mentor takes on additional responsibilities without being paid, works more than 50 hours a week, and moves from city to city.

The industry is very demanding but rewarding and appreciates those who have paid their dues so to speak. Hospitality companies are looking for confident, well-adjusted individuals with good communication and interviewing skills. To help the industry achieve its goals, many historically Black colleges and universities serve as clearing houses for qualified African-American graduates in hospitality management. This affords colleges and universities the opportunity to maintain ongoing relationships with industry personnel as well as receive constant feedback on the expectations of industry regarding entering employees.

Positioning

Position is a form of market communication that plays a vital role in enhancing the attractiveness of a tourism destination. The World Travel and Tourism Council claimed that tourism was the world's largest industry in 1991. The past few years have shown a steady increase in the volume of international travel, and along with this growth in travel, the number of tourism destination choices has also increased as many policy-makers have recognised the value of tourism to the economies of their regions. To some extent, this increased travel can also be attributed to an increase in advertising, as tourism marketers try to enlarge their share of the global tourism pie by promoting their destinations to specific target markets.

One of the most effective tools in tourism marketing is positioning. The objective of positioning is to create a distinctive place in the minds of potential customers. A position that evokes images of a destination in the customers mind; images that differentiate the destination from the competition and also as a place that can satisfy their needs and wants. Positioning is a communications strategy that is the natural follow-through of market segmentation and target marketing. Since market segmentation is based on the notion that different tourism destinations appeal to different types of tourists, target market segments must be selected before tourism marketers can begin to entice these potential customers.

An effective positioning strategy provides a competitive edge to a destination that is trying to convey its attractiveness to the target market. Positioning is more than just image creation. This important form of market communication helps to distinguish tourism destinations from similar destinations so that customers can choose the one that is the most attractive. Thus, true positioning differentiates a destination from its competitors on attributes that are meaningful to customers and gives it a competitive edge. However, this is a complex process that requires careful analysis of the attributes of destinations and the needs of the target markets.

Selection of a positioning strategy that creates a distinctive place in customers' minds is essential in preventing the following pitfalls.

1. The destination is forced into a position of competing directly with a stronger competitor. For example, a destination that is further from the source of its visitors may be relegated to a secondary or tertiary

level of competition with destinations that are closer to the market.

2. The destination's position is so unclear that its target market does not recognise the message that is being sent to them. This often happens when a destination tries to be all things to all people.
3. The destination has no identity or has a negative image in customers' minds and does not create customer demand.

Effective Positioning

According to the basic principles of marketing, products and services are created to solve customer "problems" (i.e., to satisfy needs and wants) and provide benefits. Thus, to be effective, positioning must promise the benefit the customer will receive, create the expectation, and it offer a solution to the customer's problem. If at all possible, the solution should be different from and better than the competition's solution set, especially if the competitors are already offering a similar solution.

Positioning should be a single-minded concept, an umbrella from which everything eke in the organisation flows. Properly targeted, single-minded positioning affects everything a destination does or stands for, not only advertising, but also all of its promotions. Positioning also affects policies and procedures, employee attitudes, customer relations, complaint handling, and the myriad of other details that combine to make the tourism experience. Tourism services compete on more than just image, differentiation, and benefits offered. There must be a consistency among the various offerings and it is the positioning statement that guides this consistency.

Likewise, although positioning can be applied for an entire country, a given area, or a specific city, tourism officials should develop a consistent message if the country plans to use one market to generate business for another. There are two tests of effective positioning. First, the position must be believable in the tourist's mind. Second, the destination must deliver that promise on a consistent basis.

Positioning Intangibles

One of the biggest challenges faced by tourism marketers is that the product is largely intangible. The tangibles are essential and necessary but as soon as they reach a certain level of acceptance, they become secondary. Because they are so difficult to differentiate, to be competitive, the intangibles have to be marketed. Even as tangibles, mountains and beaches have a measure of intangibility because they are experienced rather than possessed.

If tourism products are mostly intangible, they have to be marketed with tangible evidence. This is what is referred to as "tangibilising the intangible." However, this is a complicated process. By emphasising the concrete elements one may fail to differentiate oneself from the competition, and since the intangible elements are abstract, by emphasising the abstract one compounds the intangibility. Thus, tourism destination positioning should focus on enhancing and differentiating abstract realities by manipulating the tangible clues.

Unfortunately, being aware of this need does not ease the problem. It is still difficult to find meaningful tangible evidence that supports intangible constructs. What must be done, is to create a "position" in the tourist's mind. That is why positioning relies heavily on target marketing. The mental constructs held by the target market must be known, as well as the tangible evidence that sustains them. Positioning, then, is a relative term. It is not simply how the destination is perceived, but how the perceived image performs in relation to competing images. It is the customer's mental perception which may, or may not, differ from the actual physical characteristics. It is most important when, the product is an intangible and there is little difference among the competition regarding the physical characteristics.

Postitioning Process

The positioning process consists of the various steps needed to develop an effective positioning strategy. This process must be continuous to keep up with changes in the environment including the changing needs of the customer and the competitors tactics. Developing a positioning strategy for a destination in the United States to attract visitors from Japan will be used as a test case to illustrate the steps in the positioning process.

Market Positioning

Market positioning is the first step and is defined as the process of identifying and selecting markets or segments that represent business potential, to determine the criteria for competitive success. This must be based on a thorough knowledge of the needs, wants, and perceptions of the target market, along with the benefits offered by the destination.

The reality of the matter is that if the target market doesn't perceive the image, the image does not exist. If the target market does not believe that what the destination has to offer is a benefit, it isn't a benefit. If the target market doesn't believe that the benefit can be delivered, promises are meaningless. If the benefit isn't important to the target market, it isn't important. If the benefit is not perceived as being different from that of the competition, then differentiation has not succeeded. In short, images, benefits, and differentiation are solely the perception of the tourist, not the perceptions of tourism officials or the tourism marketer.

Market positioning research also requires an evaluation of the image that customers have of a tourism destination. This can be used to identify the vital elements which comprise the benefits. The beauty of a destination, the architecture of a palace, and the historic artifacts in a museum are examples of attributes that may produce a benefit, or may be a tangible representation of an intangible benefit, but are not themselves the benefit. The benefit itself is what the attributes do for the visitor, for instance, a sensation of grandeur, an aura of prestige, or the gaining of knowledge.

The credibility of these benefits may diminish rapidly if expectations are not fulfilled. Architecture is soon forgotten if the tour bus breaks down on the return trip. The impression of grandeur loses credibility if visitors feel that their personal safety is threatened. It is the fulfillment of expectations or the inability to, that creates the perception of deliverability for the tourist. Benefits, like positioning, exist in the mind of the customer and are determined only by asking the customer.

Psychological Positioning

This step utilises communications to convey a destination's identity and image to the target market. It converts customer needs into images and positions a destination in the visitors minds. Psychological positioning is a strategy employed to create a unique product image with the objective of creating interest and attracting visitors. Since it exists solely in the mind of the visitor, it can occur automatically without any effort on the part of the marketer and any kind of positioning may result.

Two very dissimilar destinations may be perceived as the same; two similar destinations may be perceived as different. What the marketer hopes to do is to control the positioning, not just let it happen. Moreover, failure to select a position in the marketplace, to achieve, and to hold that position may lead to various consequences, all undesirable, as pointed out earlier. There are two kinds of psychological positioning in marketing: objective positioning and subjective positioning.

Objective Positioning

Objective positioning is concerned, almost entirely, with the objective attributes of the physical product. It means creating an image about the destination that reflects its physical characteristics and functional features. It is usually concerned with what actually is, what exists. Objective positioning can be very important and is often used in the tourism industry. If a destination has some unique feature, that feature may be used to objectively position the destination, to create an image, and to differentiate it from the competition.

Less successful objective positioning occurs when the feature is not unique. This is why many destination promotions with pictures of beaches fail to create a distinct image or successfully differentiate the product. Other unsuccessful approaches may include a picture of two people looking at a mountain that looks like any other mountain or lying on a beach that looks like any other beach. One of the first rules of effective positioning is uniqueness.

Subjective Positioning

Subjective positioning is concerned with subjective attributes of the destination. Subjective positioning is the image, not of the physical aspects of the destination, but other attributes perceived by the tourist, (i.e., they do not necessarily belong to the destination but to the tourist's mental perception). These perceptions and the resulting images may not necessarily reflect the true state of the destination's physical characteristics. They may simply exist in the tourist's mind and not all tourists' imaging agree with a particular perception or image.

Positioning Approaches

This is the final step in the positioning process, and there are several different approaches to positioning any tourism destination. 'While psychological positioning creates an image, this positioning approach completes the picture, using visual and words, to reinforce what the destination does best and what benefits are offered. Tourism marketers may decide to select the most appropriate of the following approaches, depending on the information gathered during market and psychological positioning. Positioning by attribute, feature, or customer benefit. For this strategy, emphasis is placed on the benefits of the particular features or attributes of the destination. For example, Thailand promotes the friendliness of its people with the statement "The world meets in the land of smiles."

Price Value

International destinations are not usually positioned on the basis of price because lower prices may be perceived as connoting lower quality. However, value offered to visitors can be effectively utilised as exemplified by Malaysia which claims "Malaysia gives more natural value." With this positioning statement Malaysia is appealing not only to the sense of value (more for the money) but also to its natural attractions.

In this case, positioning features the people who should visit the destination. Hong Kong appeals to the incentive travel market with the statement 'When they've reached the top, send them to the peak,' referring to

Victoria Peak, a major tourist site in Hong Kong: Fisher Island, a luxury residential development in Florida, positions itself as the place "where people who run things can stop running."

Positioning with respect to a product class :This technique is often used to associate a destination with experiences that are extraordinary and/or unique. For example, the Principality of Monaco is positioned as "The fairy tale that does not end at midnight," or holding a convention in Thailand is 'Smooth as silk where the sky's the limit', or "If your looking for an ideal meeting place, here's one that's close to heaven" for Israel.

Positioning vis-a-vis the competition: This approach is used when it is necessary to meet the competition head-on; to bring out differences between destinations. This approach is not used frequently in international tourism destination marketing since it may involve negative statements about another country or region. However, it is regularly employed in product and services marketing. For example, Visa credit cards compete with American Express by showing examples of places from around the world that do not accept American Express and only Visa cards are accepted.

Positioning is the ultimate weapon in niche marketing. Positioning is a valuable weapon for tourism marketers. To position successfully requires recognising the marketplace, the competition, and tourists' perceptions. Posi-tioning analysis on a target market basis provides the tools to identify opportunities for creating the desired image that differentiates a destination from its competitors and for serving the target market better than anyone else.

Search Engine Marketing

Search engines are as pervasive as the Internet. Google is now a public company with a market cap of $80 billion;

MSN launched a new search engine; AOL announces the creation of its own search engine; and traditional marketing budgets are being rewritten for search marketing and the web. In recent years research firms have begun studying the influence of search on consumer behaviour, and its impact on the travel industry. They have identified online users as only somewhat satisfied with search results and are willing to switch from one search engine to another showing very little loyalty.

Unlike other e-commerce categories, Internet users search for travel and hospitality services and offerings within the context of the destination. Therefore the search engine strategy for travel and hotel websites is subject to a different methodology than what the generalist SEO (Search Engine Optimisation) companies offer. Marketing a bank, eyeglass store, or dental office does not factor the characteristics or intensity of the destination. Nor do generalists differentiate travel search behaviors from general online consumers.

A destination-focused search engine strategy requires in-depth knowledge of the travel and hospitality industry, extensive destination research, destination target keyword analysis, and destination search behaviour. Only a destination-focused search engine strategy can help the travel and hotel website leverage the popularity of the destination to its benefit. With such vast numbers of searches originating from search engines, clearly search engines are an essential component to the hotel's direct online distribution strategy. Ranking high on the engines and consistently staying there along with matching the right budget to compete effectively are all major competitive issues with advertisers online.

Over the last year or so, a new term, "Golden Triangle" has entered the search marketing vernacular. Novel research using beams of light that bounce off the eyeballs of online test users and onto a conditioned computer screen, captured certain patterns of online viewing behaviour when on search engines. The highest concentration of visualisations appeared on the top three to four listings in the natural listings and top one to two in the sponsored listings. Basically a triangle began to form as more people tended to look in this top corner of the page now referred to in search marketing as the "Golden Triangle."

In hospitality, search marketing is part of your online distribution strategy. We have all become travel agents with our desktop, laptop, PDA, or other electronic devises and the strategy is to reach your specific customer segments when they are searching for you. Lodging companies that do not have the marketing budget of the major intermediaries must rely even more on search engine referrals. Therefore good positioning of your hotel website on the major search engines is of critical importance and can directly affect your bottom line.

Search Marketing

Search marketing is only one of the many aspects of a robust eMarketing strategy. An effective eMarketing strategy in hospitality utilises all the market resources and channels available on the Internet. This includes implementing robust search engine marketing, email capture and email marketing, link creation and link popularity strategy, online sponsorships, display advertising, and much more. eMarketing and its various formats can be used successfully as a direct response vehicle (short-term, results-oriented) or as a branding tool (long-term and meets strategic goals).

Due to budget limitations, seasonal demand and the perishable character of hotel inventories, HeBS usually recommends that hoteliers focus their resources on eMarketing formats that are best used as a direct response tool:

— Search Engine Marketing

— Email Marketing

— Link Popularity

— Online Sponsorships

Search Engine Marketing begins by making the site represent best practices in website optimisation. This includes turning the hotel website into a search engine-friendly website, enhancing the relevancy and richness of the content, developing customer segmentation, incorporating a destination web strategy, performing relevant keyword search analysis, boosting the keyword density of the visible copy, developing page titles, description and meta tags, performing search engine registrations, launching search marketing campaigns in all search formats, and making sure site is constructed in such as that is friendly to the search engines.

Search engine marketing has five unique aspects:

Natural listings

Natural search is the most popular type. Contrary to popular belief natural (organic) listings are not free. Good search engine rankings of your website require extensive, ongoing website optimisation efforts that have to be budgeted. But this is definitely the most inexpensive form of search marketing in the long run as optimising the site is a long term investment in the site. The search engines serve up natural listings using ever changing algorithmic formulas, whose composition is a closely guarded secret.

These algorithms are based on different number of variables for each search engine, over 100 in the case of Google. Some of the variables are: website navigation and architecture, relevancy of contents, keyword density, link popularity, meta tags, description tags, page titles, Traffic rank, Page Rank, fresh content, activity and traffic on the website, and many more.

Website optimisation vs. search engine optimisation

Direct Online Distribution begins and ends with the hotel website. A well functioning, fully optimised website is a real asset that serves as the chief instrument to capture new markets and facilitate transactions, and communicate with a) your customers and b) with the search engines. Many hotel websites are performing poorly as far as online distribution and search engine strategy are concerned. Why? Many hotel websites have been developed by web designers who know nothing about the hospitality industry, based on input and concepts by hoteliers who are not experts on Internet strategy, online distribution, and eMarketing. And many of them were designed as online brochures without taking into account principles in fundamental search engine marketing and online distribution.

Using a "quick fix" approach

Such hotel websites inevitably produce poor results and few bookings. Hoteliers then turn to Search Engine Optimisation (SEO) vendors for a quick fix of the hotel website to boost search engine rankings and increase online revenues. In reality, "slapping" meta tags to a stale, user and search engine unfriendly website and submitting it to the search engines can achieve few sustainable results.

Good search engine rankings require systematic, ongoing website optimisation. Only a fully optimised website developed according to the best practices in online distribution and marketing can produce robust revenues, top search engine rankings, and position your hotel company ahead of the competition. Website optimisation takes a comprehensive look at the website and prepares it for optimal performance (maximum user experience, bookability and conversion rates) and yes, the search engines.

Website optimisation to the rescue

·Website Optimisation often starts by undoing damaged work of web designers and SEO firms. One must recognise that Website Optimisation rather than Search Engine Optimisation takes a total review of the website from the way it was built to expansion of navigation, to revamping and building keyword rich body copy. Website Optimisation includes among other things: optimising the architecture of the site, introducing tiered navigation on the site, optimising the body copy and drastically increasing the "Keyword Density" of the site, introducing rich content addressing all of the key customer segments, turning your hotel into the "hero" of the destination, creating landing pages for various email marketing and PPC marketing campaigns, enriching the website with relevant and fresh content and act as additional entry points to the site, boosting the Traffic Rank of the site, launching a comprehensive Link Popularity strategy for the website, and yes, optimising the page titles, description and meta tags to support the body copy.

Here are the most important criteria used by the search engines to rank a hotel website:

— The overall search-engine friendliness of the site:

— The search engine bots do not like sites built entirely in FLASH, sites built in frames, Intro/ Splash pages with no navigation and copy, lack of site maps, the copy in GIF or JPEG and not in HTML text format, poor body copy, and lack of relevant contents, etc)

— Rich and relevant content on the site
— Body copy with high Keyword Density
— Invisible copy (page titles, description tags, meta tags) that supports the visible (body copy)
— Link Popularity of the site (number of incoming links from highly authoritative websites like hotel directories, portals, etc)
— PageRank (Google)
— Traffic Rank

As a result of their assessment the search engines determine the relevancy of the website to each keyword used to decide the ranking of the site.

Body Copy

The copy on the hotel website serves two audiences: the Internet users and the search engines. The body copy plays an essential role in promoting the hotel and its product/services to the web customers. Equally important is that today's search engines value the descriptive body copy found on the web page. The body copy must contain relevant target keywords and phrases (destination and product related) that permeate throughout the website.

Search engines rate body copy as the only truthful source to pull descriptive data on the website for indexing. Search engine executives constantly reiterate that the body copy is the most important factor for getting high rankings. Search engines value the descriptive body copy (visible copy) found on the website more than the invisible copy (tags). The body copy must contain relevant target keywords and phrases (destination and product related) that permeate throughout the website.

The so called "Keyword Density" i.e. number of keywords per 100 words of copy should be enhanced significantly. Search engines rate body copy as the only truthful source to pull descriptive data on the website for indexing. Search engine executives constantly reiterate, the body copy is the most important factor for getting high rankings.

Link Popularity

Link popularity is another important criteria used by the search engines (Google, Yahoo, MSN, etc) when ranking a website. The higher the link popularity, the more authoritative and relevant the incoming links, the better the chances for a top position in the search engine results. Link popularity refers to the number and quality of incoming links that are pointing to the website. Outside websites that consider your own website important will create a link to your site. In the search engines' view, links to your website are considered important. Each link is considered a "vote of confidence" by a third party website for your site.

Today search engines want links from authoritative sites, or links from websites that share the same focus as your website, i.e. travel-related websites, destination portals, travel guides, CVBs, travel and hotel directories, etc. Positioning the hotels on such authoritative sites achieves two goals:

— Boosts its Link Popularity which is vital for the search engine rankings

— Leverages the marketing dollars and accumulated traffic of these sites, which ultimately will increase direct sales as more traffic is led toward the brand website.

The goal is for the hotel to position itself at all "points of contact" with potential Internet travel bookers. Utilised expertly, these important online channels can produce immediate results, while keeping the hotel company and properties in full control of the brand, pricing strategy and revenue management techniques. An essential by-product of such a strategy is the incoming link generation by outside websites.

Paid Inclusion

Paid Inclusion is an alternative method to appearing on the search engines in the natural listings. By registering specified URLs through Paid Inclusion, these pages become catalogued and indexed every more frequently. Paid Inclusion is ideal for pages rich with keyword density copy or copy that changes frequently. When keywords are searched, the listing appears in the organic listing and the click is a fixed price of 15 to 30 cents, depending upon which service used. Listings in the Paid Inclusion services are the result of less passive and slightly more aggressive methods of introducing new pages and auditing and enhancing existing in order to further boost appearance in the natural listings.

Pay Per Click Marketing

PPC listings are not served by the search engines as natural listings as the two search types mentioned above but in a separate category typically under "Sponsored Links." Pay-per-click (PPC) or Pay-for- performance services as they are sometimes known have become extremely popular and are a smart way to position your hotel as "Sponsored Links" or enhanced listings in the search engine results. Over 50% of every online advertising dollar in 2005 will be spent on PPC and paid-inclusion vs. less than 20% on display advertising (e.g. banner ads).

PPC is the most aggressive way to influence your appearance on the search engines. HeBS foresees increasing importance of this search marketing format and considers it as a major short to mid-term distressed inventory disposal tool:

— Direct-to-consumer channel
— Customers visit and book on hotel website
— Preserves Brand Integrity
— Ideal distressed hotel inventory disposal tool
— Captures new customer segments
— Takes advantage of local events and happenings
— Free impressions-great branding effect at no cost

Local Search

Local search has gained strong momentum as more consumers become accustomed to conducting destination oriented searches, especially when the destination is significant as with the travel industry. All of the major search engines have introduced Local Search functionality (e.g. Yahoo, Google, etc). Local Search marketing can pursue several simultaneous avenues: local search directory listings, online yellow pages enhanced listings, local search PPC campaigns, etc.

Local searches enable businesses to increase sales by precisely targeting customers interested in your neighbourhood who are searching on the Internet for local products and services, whether your hotel has a website or not. With an emphasis on local searches the impact on the hospitality industry is obvious. All travel is destination oriented and requires a local address. Savvy hoteliers can definitely take advantage of this marketing format and stay ahead of the competition.

The so called Travel Search Engines facilitate comparison shopping by compiling results from various sources and provide a price comparison of the product searched. This allows the shopper to check rates and availability of different providers on one website.

Once a search is requested, the data displays a number of supplier + intermediary sites with rates for same dates of availability. The business model is advertising model combined with a standard commission per sale or advertising model combined with a pay per click model much like the traditional PPC services. In online retail, comparison shopping has been around for at least 8 years, so the experiences in this sector are indicative of what would happen in the travel sector.

To a great extent the online intermediaries like Expedia and Travelocity feel threatened by this business model and are reluctant to participate in this new type of Travel Search Engines. On the other hand seasoned online travellers treat the online intermediaries as travel search engines and use them to comparison shop. A recent survey by PhoCusWright finds that four out of ten online travel shoppers have shopped on online intermediary sites, but ultimately purchased direct from a supplier.

Based on the history of comparison shopping in online retail, current realities in the marketplace (suppliers maintain strict rate parity and best internet rate guarantees), well established online purchasing habits, and other factors, HeBS does not believe that travel search engines can gain widespread recognition and acceptance in the marketplace. We expect only a few of the existing players to remain in the long haul. Comparison shopping has always been a very narrow niche market.

Email Marketing

In the context of explosive growth in Internet distribution and marketing in hospitality, email marketing is a powerful direct-to-consumer distribution and marketing tool. It allows hoteliers to engage customers in strong, personalised and mutually beneficial interactive relationships, increases conversions, and sells more efficiently.

Email marketing is an important aspect of today's multi-channel marketing model that requires hoteliers to communicate a single brand image across all channels. Email marketing spending will triple from $2.1 billion in 2003 to $6.1 billion in 2008, according to Jupiter Research forecast. By segment expenses are committed to newsletter sponsorships, outsourced email delivery, and the email list rental, which will continue to outpace the other two combined. In hospitality, email marketing continues to receive marketers' attention because costs remain relatively low, it is easy and fun to create and to implement and the results can be measured practically in real time.

Intuitively, email marketing makes sense-email creates direct revenue opportunities with past, present, and future customers. Email marketing's ease of use also means more email clutter. According to DoubleClick, in the past year delivery rates have increased by 1.5% while open and click-through rates have declined by 5.6%. Growing competition for attention makes all our jobs more difficult. Click through rates for travel remains steady and equal to the industry average of 8.4%. Your campaigns should equal or exceed the CTR of 8.4%.

Permission-based email remains strongest for consumer readership, general satisfaction, and likelihood to purchase, according to a study by NOP World Research, 2004. Response rates to satisfaction, likelihood to purchase, and recommend to others were 10 percentage points higher for recipients of permission based email than unsolicited emails.

Designing your Email Marketing Strategy

Following are some important considerations when designing your Email Marketing Strategy

Know Your Customer: Knowing your customers is an extremely important consideration when conceptualising and designing your hotel email marketing strategy. Addressing your key audiences and providing them with relevant information is one of the key aspects of any successful email marketing campaign.

It is a matter of perspective on what is truly important to the customer. Different characteristics of the property and its product can appeal to different customer segments. For example, to the business traveller, choosing a hotel may be influenced by the availability of a function room, high-speed Internet access or proximity to an area corporation, while a leisure traveller may find the same hotel attractive because of its great location near local area attractions and family friendly entertainment. Same hotel, same destination, but different appeal requiring differentiated email marketing message.

Create a Single-View Email List: Are all customer emails and relevant guest data from POS, PMS, CRS, call center and Web channelled into a single email database? A single-view customer database has obvious benefits:

— Allows you to establish a single and easy to manage opt-in email list

— Allows you to address all of your customer segments

— Perform ongoing and frequent updates to the email database

— Use an appending service to obtain the email addresses of past guests for whom you only have a physical address.

— Identify your most valuable customers with best lifetime value perspective (80:20 principle)

— Launch email campaigns addressing different customer segments by adjusting a "master template"

Email marketing is a crucial component of the hotel's overall eMarketing and online distribution strategy. The shift toward online purchasing means that the hotel website is becoming the "first point of entry" to establish interactive relationships with your customers. Capturing client email profiles on your website has become increasingly important.

The hotel is in a unique position to build a robust email list from existing customers. When using your own email list to market the hotel, the conversion rates can be 15-20 times greater than any stand-alone rented mailing list because the targeted group already knows and has experienced your product first-hand. In addition, the hotel can stratify the customer list by specific characteristics, communicate and offer value in the message, and send targeted and relevant mailings frequently to the intended audience who may even anticipate these messages.

The property should also consider additional means to capture emails at the property level: at the front desk and the PMS level, by introducing free promotions, customer surveys, and email data cards to name a few. With the right capture strategy and a coordinated and combined effort by the front desk and sales staff, the email customer list can grow rapidly into a robust direct distribution channel. For the actual email capture and email list functionality, consider using any of the many third party email vendor that provides low cost tools to capture, maintain, secure, and enforce the recent CAN-SPAM laws. These vendors provide templates and reporting tools to track and measure email campaigns.

Testing Your Email Campaign : As with any marketing campaign you want to be certain your message is clear and effective. For email, the subject line is critical as it serves a dual purpose of summarising the content of the email and entices the recipient to open and read more. As email clutter grows the subject line becomes even more important. Once there was a time when the email simply dropped into the email box. Now you have to contend with spam screeners, virus protectors, and skeptical consumers. Assume the email gets passed these filters and drops into the email box, now subject line prominently appears to the reader.

The subject line will determine the success of the entire campaign. It serves as the hook for the reader to bite on. To measure the validity of the campaign before a full launch, conduct your very own focus group. Take a sampling of customers from your database and test the sales message as it appears in the subject line. Narrow your choice to three different versions of the message and use the click-to-view and click-through rates to determine which sales message drew the greatest response.

Goals in Email Marketing

Internet marketing and email marketing in particular can be used successfully as a direct response vehicle (short-term, results-oriented) or as a branding tool (long-term and strategic goals). The best measure of any hotel marketing campaign—email or other—is the number of new reservations generated by the campaign. With a special rate code embedded in the email-only offer or use of a special 1-800 number can provide the means to track the results.

Since the science of marketing is also to influence purchasing habits and create future demand, a more realistic measure is the general impact created in the campaign not just immediate reservations. The analytics to measure the success of an email campaign should include: open or view rates, click through rates, the number of pages viewed, the duration of the site visit, the number of contact forms submitted, the number of phone calls received, revenues and roomnights from special rate code bookings or packages purchased, and the long term sustainability of the campaign.

A marketing promotion is a call to action. You create the sales message for the consumer to react soon if not immediately. The challenge through email is to solicit a response amidst competing solicitations from other travel and non travel related products. Once the campaign is launched the buzz around the message already begins the fade. It is that simple. The buzz tapers off the further we get from the date of the message announcement. At least with direct mail a postcard or brochure may sit on the kitchen table in clear view for weeks before the recipient acts.

The influence of an email decays based on the rate of new email arrivals. After 72 hours studies have shown the email becomes completely forgotten. Timing has become an important issue for email, not just for the best time to launch a campaign but the window of opportunity to act on the sale. According to a study by eMail Labs in coordination with eMarketer, an Internet marketing research group, email campaigns enjoy the best view and click-through rates, as high as 22.8 percent, on Wednesday and Thursday. So intuitively launch the campaign in the late morning or early afternoon, after the overnight junk mail has been cleared, if you are trying to reach people at their work desk.

Consider placing a time constraint on the sales message. A real or artificial expiration date motivates the recipient to act. The timeliness of your appeal also turns a simple promotion from common to premium and ordinary into unique and special in the recipient's mind. It prompts them to act. An entire industry of last-minute, 11th hour services now live off the exclusivity of your perishable inventory. Nothing stops the hotelier from doing the same by using email marketing.

eFaxing

With complaints of spam and email clutter, fax marketing presents an interesting opportunity for the hotel marketer. It is an excellent option, particularly with a robust fax database. Through faxes you can distribute your sales message to the intended audience. Some of the better third party email vendors offer the eFax functionality as part of their total email toolkit and are keen to help adhere to any fax spam rules. In fact, such vendors allow you to send either a fax or email as back up if the first delivery method fails.

Since faxing is a phone based system, expect a phone delivery charge of around 8-12 cents in the U.S. and higher for international calls. Fax reporting capabilities are limited to the delivery rate since there is no other automated tracking mechanism like with email. However, a unique rate in the sales message can help measure the campaign's efficacy.

Personalisation

Personalisation is more than providing the right information to the right person at the right time. Personalising of the eMarketing message is a powerful conversion and retention tool. Customising your interaction with your most valuable customers (those 20% that generate 80% of your business) will provide significant long-term rewards.

Personalisation on the property level should start by identifying all "electronic touch points" with your customers (hotel guests, meeting planners, travel professionals, etc) and creating an action plan. Personalise all electronic communications with your customers. Every email guru expounds on the importance of personalisation. If you have the name, use it and use it wherever possible, in the greeting and in the subject line. True, such personalisation smells like the work of spammers because they are the most adept at using technology, but the name coupled with a recognisable hotel name and enticing subject line can boost your open and click-through dramatically.

Synergy

A landing page is a web page that was linkable from an email message. Too often, however, the email message and the landing page are not synergistic. Too often the home page serves as the landing page for all promotional messages in the email. This creates as much confusion as it does frustration to the reader.

The message and landing page must be synergistic. With a content management system (CMS), the hotel marketer can create new pages in real time as the email gets created. By matching each sales promotion in the email message to a relevant link for more information, you have streamlined the reading process for the recipient. The user can now go directly to the site for more information specific about the package or special in the email and complete the transaction.

Spam Filters

Thought leaders, including Bill Gates, have suggested a number of archaic initiatives to curb spam. These include a charge per email similar to a postage stamp, a bond in escrow drawn down based on email sender violations, and the blacklisting of IP addresses. The Sender Policy Framework (SPF), an anti-spam approach which authenticates the sender before mailing, has drawn both successes and mailers in test markets.

Merchant Model

Over the last 4 years many hoteliers have been struggling to decrease their dependence on the online merchants and to develop direct online distribution strategies of their own. Hoteliers are also trying to find answers to several critical questions: does the cost of doing business with online merchants outweigh the cost of not doing business with them? While hoteliers gave up rooms at steep discounts, online merchants became darlings on Wall Street.

The Internet is all about transparency, efficient distribution of information, and inexpensive e-commerce transactions. It is the most efficient marketing and distribution medium ever invented. It is simply the best direct-to-consumer distribution channel ever created and it definitely favours supplier-buyer relationships. Nowhere is this better illustrated than between hotel and customer.

Hoteliers that embraced their own direct online distribution efforts first and merchants second now enjoy as much as 40% to 60% of total revenues from their own websites. In this sense the abnormally high margins of the merchant model (18% to 30%) constitute a temporary anomaly, not the rule. That is because the merchant model contradicts the very nature of the Internet as an efficient and direct-to-consumer channel. The marketplace cannot tolerate deficiencies and abnormally high profit margins except on a temporary basis in periods of major industry transitions or during the emergence of entirely new distribution and marketing media (i.e. the Internet).

Travel is all about selling a dream, an anticipated experience. Selling a hotel stay over the Web does not require warehouses, complicated wholesale and retail arrangements or fulfillment centers. Hoteliers know their product, destination, and customers better than anybody else. Just think about what a smart hotelier can do by employing rich media on the Web (virtual tours, photo galleries, floor plans, interactive applications, etc). In this sense to market well online hoteliers do not need third party intermediaries, and can do the job themselves.

The proverbial pendulum has shifted back in favour of hoteliers. Major brands and savvy hoteliers are re-gaining control of the online distribution channel and have already proven that they can dictate the terms of the online game via tight control over properties, rate parity, best rate guarantees and successful loyalty programmes.

The merchant model, used as the main business model by leading online intermediaries, is becoming more flexible due to the changing market conditions and increased pressure by travel suppliers: corporate contracts, lower mark-ups (e.g. 18%-22%), direct interfaces to the major brand CRSs, and last room availability on the hotel site. All of these concessions would have been unthinkable just two years ago.

This trend will inevitably accelerate over the next years as travel suppliers and major hotel brands continue to apply pressure on the online intermediaries in an environment of improved economic conditions and positive changes in consumer purchasing behaviour. The online merchants are embracing the dynamic packaging model as the next high profit margin generator. The agency model is beginning to regain at least some of its past luster as a result of the rate parity introduced by all major brands, and the lower merchant mark-ups negotiated by some of the major hotel brands.

Future Developments in Hospitality

Hospitality eBusiness Strategies firmly believes that the following crucial developments in the hospitality industry over the next five years will benefit hoteliers and other travel suppliers and help lessen their dependence on the online intermediaries and transform the merchant model as we know it:

In 2005 over 25% of all hotel room revenue will be booked online. Another 25% of hotel bookings will be directly influenced by the Internet but done offline. In 2006 this percentage will exceed 27% to 29%. Overall travel booked online will exceed 31% to 35% of total bookings over the next 2 years.

From the major brands to savvy hotel management companies (HMC) to the individual hotel owner operator, each is firmly gaining control of their relationships with the third parties, and have instituted preferred or approved partner programmes (similar to IHG). Franchisee direct contracts with the online intermediaries will disappear and will be folded into the corporate agreements with preferred or approved third parties.

HMCs with multiple properties in the same destination can offer consumers a choice of hotels with their own destination sites, and independents are becoming increasingly choosy and very careful with their third-party relationships. The overall trend is to work with fewer, "hotel friendlier" and carefully chosen online intermediaries.

Major hotel brands and many savvy hoteliers already operate in a rate parity and best rate guarantee environment and will continue to do so in the foreseeable future. In the near future major brands and smart hoteliers will start introducing restrictions on how net wholesale rates can be marketed on the Internet by the third parties, which will gradually lead to a requirement that net rates should be bundled with other services and cannot be exposed "naked" on the Web.

Online intermediaries will further embrace and perfect the dynamic packaging model thus turning themselves into typical online wholesale packagers/tour operators. Dynamic packaging and the addition of local sightseeing and entertainment will be the only chance of the online intermediaries to generate higher profit margins. In addition to the dynamic packaging model which will become the norm, the online intermediaries will embrace the advertising model and start offering enhanced listings and positioning, pay-per-click (PPC) and display advertising programmes, to supplement their decreased margins.

8

Shared Services in the Hospitality

Finance and accounting functions have become a primary target for scrutiny by the hospitality industry. A centralised or regionalised "shared service center" offers one of the most significant areas of opportunity for some hotel organisations. Under a shared services model, information processing traditionally split between headquarters and the individual hotel properties can be done on an organisation-wide basis at a central facility.

Business functions—including general accounting, accounts payable, accounts receivable, fixed asset management, purchasing and month-end closing procedures—can be decentralised functions within the hospitality industry. These day-to-day functions are repetitive in nature, and economies of scale may be realised by utilising a shared services concept. A shared service center has the potential to serve hotel properties positioned globally with benefits including faster processing, improved customer service and lower costs due to reduced personnel. Design and implementation of a shared service center, however, raise critical issues for a hotel organisation both from a technology and a change management perspective.

The traditional hotel company, comprised of owned, managed, and franchised properties has historically located accounting and finance employees at the property level, as well as at the corporate office. Traditionally all financial information has been sent to the corporate office for consolidation, data analysis and reporting, although the primary processing has taken place at the property level.

Often, the different systems being used at the individual hotels have resulted in inefficiencies at the corporate level with many manual processes being required, including data re-entry, in order to complete a consolidation and prepare the necessary executive information. The relatively antiquated and cumbersome information systems at the corporate headquarters have further hindered the ability of users to receive information in a timely and cost-efficient manner.

A number of the major hotel companies are either considering or are already moving towards implementation of a shared services system. Factors driving this decision include a desire for growth, the need to outperform the competition, and the desire to satisfy both the company's guests and individual hotel owners. All of these factors—coupled with a need to reduce overhead costs—makes shared services a viable solution.

The shared services model can help to lower processing costs, create a customer-driven "center of excellence," consolidate multiple processing locations into one location and incorporate a "fee for service" approach to transaction processing. This model is geared towards repetitive transactions that can be somewhat automated or handled through mass processing. Personnel can be consolidated and spend more time on "value-added" tasks under this model. Management will then be able to spend more time on making informed decisions, as meaningful data will be more readily available.

CENTRALISATION

Centralisation, however, introduces several new business challenges which must be addressed prior to implementing a shared services system, with the selection of current technology to support a new structure being one of the most important. The many pieces in the technology puzzle include the architecture required to support the central functions, the application software needed to best handle data processing and reporting, and the communication requirements between the service center and remote locations.

Each site will need its own Local Area Network (LAN), which will then be connected to the Wide Area Network (WAN). The WAN will connect all remote sites to the central service center, and the central service center to the corporate headquarters if they are separated geographically, and allow users to access data for the entire enterprise as appropriate. To access the data, communication lines from each remote site to the service center database will need to be in place.

The application software is also very important in the infrastructure of the service center. It needs to be functionally rich and powerful enough to handle processing and reporting for multiple entities which may have very different requirements. For example, a resort hotel may need to track more detail than a small hotel with no restaurants, and institutional owners may need different reports than a developer/owner. The system must track an abundance of information, but also be capable of segregating the information so that management can access only the key results they need. Management must have extensive on-line data access and reporting tools to assist them in decision-making and business planning.

Within the technology challenge, system security becomes an issue. When accounting functions including payables and receivables are being processed by a service center which is handling numerous owner's accounts, data integrity becomes a primary concern. A system needs multiple levels of security to ensure that data is secured, that appropriate access is granted only to the people who should handle the data and that audit trails are available for researching any discrepancies.

Costs and Savings

Possibly the biggest challenge in centralising transaction processing is determining the costs and savings from creating a shared service structure. Costs can range from new hardware and software purchases to relocation costs of employees reassigned to work in the service center. The costs must be allocated to those who will benefit from and receive services from the new center. The costs for the shared services model are easier to identify than the savings. The initial investment in the service center includes:

— Application hardware and software;
— The WAN and LAN costs;
— Rent and building improvements;
— Employee relocation and severance expense;
— Initial training and change management;
— Implementing the new structure.

The on-going costs include the training and procedure development, communication costs, payroll and other overhead expenses. The benefits of a service center are more difficult to assess than the costs as many are intangible, including the potential for providing easier access to more meaningful data. A shared service center also may result in more informed decision-making and an infrastructure capable of supporting increased growth.

Placing a dollar value on such benefits can be difficult. Other benefits, however, can be more readily quantified, including:

— Reduced total head count;
— Processing time per transaction;
— Improved customer service response times;
— Improved average days to collect outstanding receivables.

Depending on the current environment and the number of repetitive tasks, the savings will vary. Companies that depend on manual processing or have outdated information systems can realise the greatest savings. Companies that have numerous locations that handle the same types of transactions can also realise big savings. Economically, the shared services model can work. Initial investments can be allocated on a pro-rata share basis to each participating location. Ongoing costs can also be allocated based either on a "fee-for-service" basis or a flat annual fee. Along with the savings, these allocations make the centralisation structure a cost reduction tool for many organisations.

Companies adopting a centralised process structure under a shared service model often implement change management efforts along with new information systems. Together, the two initiatives create an environment for reducing operating costs and improving efficiencies. In developing a strategy for a shared service center, a phased approach is preferable. The first phase calls for a Conference Room Pilot (CRP), which involves a minimal set-up of the new hardware and software at corporate headquarters, and one or two remote properties brought on line to test the entire design.

Corporate implementation is followed by the second phase, the enterprise-wide roll-out. The CRP phase is designed to identify unique requirements and assess the risks associated with the service center concept. Detailed requirements, confirmation and design will be completed during this phase. The technical architecture will be implemented, selected business scenarios tested and change management efforts developed during the CRP. As part of the change management efforts, all newly centralised processes will be redefined. Workflow will be streamlined and current job descriptions will be revamped while new job descriptions are being defined.

During the next phase, Service Center Implementation, change management and process improvement implementation efforts will be the main focus. Newly defined processing methods will be implemented. All remaining untested business scenarios will be tested. Data conversion and testing will take place. The center will then go online and processing will begin. The next phase, Remote Location Implementation, will consist of the same implementation efforts from the previous phase, but will focus on the individual hotels.

During this phase, an implementation team approach will be utilised. Small, highly focused teams will go to each remote location to quickly implement the centralised structure and bring them up on the new system. Change management will also be very important as the move to a shared service center often results in significant changes in the way the accounting and finance function is conducted at the hotel. In particular, the role of the hotel controller will likely undergo major change.

All locations need to be involved in the process of developing and implementing a shared service center. This was the most valuable lesson learned during the analysis of centralisation versus decentralisation in information processing. Determining what functions to handle at the local level—in contrast to the service center—was one of the most difficult tasks. Without assistance from the individual locations, decisions would be made in a vacuum reflecting only the perspective of the corporate headquarters.

To be successful, organisations need early buy-in from both management and staff personnel in all areas within the company. The more involved each project team member is, the smoother and more valuable the transition will be. Clearly, hotel companies need to review their operations as they seek to manage properties better, cheaper and more efficiently. The shared services model offers great potential, particularly for large hotel companies with operations scattered across distant locations.

Cost savings from more efficient transaction processing can be significant, freeing capital currently used in "back-office" operations for other purposes, including strategic growth. In addition, a shared service center also creates the foundation for improved information available for management decision-making and customer service. In this way, a shared service center can contribute in a direct and material way to a hotel company's competitive advantage.

Programme of System Integration

In hospitality, the responsibility for a company's growth is frequently relegated to the sales and marketing people who must find ways to fill the additional rooms. This is often the case even if the expansion adds questionable new inventory to a brand struggling for consistency -or in the face of the company's preoccupation with other priorities. The ability of the sales and marketing team to deliver business and the operations people to produce bottom-line results will often depend on a well-orchestrated programme of system integration that improves efficiency, increases productivity and supports higher guest-service standards, particularly in a multi-property environment.

In producing a "systems solution," the challenge is to make technology work in a truly integrated way. Traditional technology offerings tend to be architected for a single function (i.e., point-of-sale, food & beverage, security and the like) and mostly for a single property. Often these systems operate on multiple hardware and software platforms. Typically, these systems have not provided the necessary level of integration, having been developed without using progressive "open system" client/server concepts.

Consolidating and sharing data across properties was never considered during design and implementation of these individual systems. In the aftermath of a new business combination or multi-property development, a system approach must be considered, but only at the appropriate functionality and at the right price. And when it comes to making these choices, both functionality and price depend on the company's strategic business plan and organisational design. Three primary technology options are available: development of a Superbase, a shared-service center or a hybrid integration of these two approaches.

"Superbase" Approach

For those companies willing to forego some functionality to maintain a lower cost structure, a system approach may include designing a wide area network (WAN) to an already existing local area network (LAN) at the property level. This approach provides a one-way information download from the property unit to a central site that incorporates a centralised super-database (Superbase), which connects the individual properties via a WAN. Each property's LAN essentially becomes a node on the cross-property WAN. The Superbase contains mini-databases for hotel gaming, and property transactions.

Either an Enterprise Resource Planning (ERP) system or an optional data warehouse could integrate the data by combining it from each of the other databases, providing a means for three-dimensional data cubing and transaction analysis. Prior to making the trek across the WAN to the Superbase, the data is accumulated in staging areas (located on each LAN), then translated and standardised into a common data format.

The solution is simplified if all of the properties to be linked share a common technological infra-structure. This is rarely the case, however. Once the data is in the Superbase, it becomes part of a set of databases. Getting the data to the Superbase in a common format, however, can be quite a challenge. This can be achieved by using a "universal translator" attached to the staging area on each LAN. This translator converts the data from the individual systems into a format that is used by the Superbase and is designed to be flexible enough to easily incorporate the constant flux of changes that the individualised systems go through in their lifetime.

The Superbase concept allows each property to maintain its individual systems with minimal cost overhead. The wide area network (WAN) provides the holding area for multi-property data. The WAN file server can be located at one of the properties or at the corporate office. As a result, there are few organisational changes and investment outlays. In addition, the Superbase is designed to be expandable. If a new data stream is added to a property, it would not be a major technological undertaking requiting several months of development work to link to the Superbase.

A translation protocol to interpret and standardise the data -and space on the Superbase to store it—is all that would be required. The data residing on the Superbase can also be easily funneled into a data warehouse for three —dimensional financial and marketing analysis. One of the biggest disadvantages to the Superbase is illustrated by the casino example in Scenario One. For the cross-property comp information to be used, it must be viewed on the Superbase, which is limited by the one-way interface from the property LAN to the WAN. In addition, the Superbase requires clearly defined business rules agreed upon by all properties as a result of consolidating data using one standardised approach.

Scenario One

Setting

A corporation owns three gaming properties in the same metropolitan area. Each property has varying technological infrastructures handling its data, but corporate management allows guests to combine credit redemption points so that they may be used across the three properties.

Scenario

A customer gambles at Casino I then visits Casino 2 where he or she also plays. The customer has earned enough combined value from gambling at both casinos to earn a free meal at a buffet. Eager for a new environment, the customer ventures to Casino 3 to redeem the buffet.

Problem

Several different transactions have to be made to three distinct systems at the three properties: one transaction to debit the complementary value (or "comp") from Casino I; one transaction to debit the comp value from Casino 2; one transaction to credit the player's account at Casino 3 so he or she can receive the free buffet; and finally, a last transaction to debit the player's account at Casino 3 for the amount of the buffet. This can become an accounting and reporting nightmare for each property. Since financial reporting can be quite slow, it may be days before the guest's account shows the correct account balance. Until the correct information is shown, the guest may potentially redeem his points again at the other casinos while waiting for the accounting system to catch up.

One-way Integration Solution

The solution to this scenario lies in the Superbase design and one of its primary components the sub-database containing the redemption transaction data. This sub-database is the centralised repository for all point and comp information. Using the proposed cross-property solution, casino managers who plan to market across their properties will no longer be able to manage comps from the individual property's casino management system. To assure that the proper accounts balance and the correct reporting structure is maintained in a real-time manner, all comp transactions must be initiated from the Superbase.

Two-Way Integration—Shared Service Center Approach

The second system integration approach addresses the concerns of the especially complex organisations that need to manage and manipulate enterprise-wide data with functionality extending to both property and corporate sites. This approach offers a two-way solution that is most often developed through a shared-service center design. While the upfront investment associated with this second option may be costly, the long-term return for a shared-service center may outweigh the short-term outlays - if the organisation and its respective properties can reach the required economies of scale.

Business functions, especially those in the finance and accounting arena, are prime candidates for a shared-service concept given the repetitive nature of these processes. Hospitality companies comprising a mix of owned, managed, and franchised properties have historically had accounting and finance employees at the corporate office, as well as at the property level.

All financial information has typically been sent to the corporate office for consolidation, data analysis and reporting although the primary process has taken place at the property level. The different systems and processes used at individual hotels have often resulted in inefficiencies at the corporate level with many manual processes being required, including data re-entry to complete a consolidation and prepare the necessary executive information.

Scenario Two presents an example of solutions in a shared-services approach. In a multi-property environment, the shared - services model can help to lower processing costs, create a customer -driven "center of excellence," consolidate multiple processing locations into one location and incorporate a "fee for service" approach to transaction processing.

Similar to the one-way and hybrid integration approach, each site will need its own LAN, which will then be connected to the WAN. The WAN will connect all remote sites to the central service center and allow users to access data for the entire enterprise as appropriate. To access the data, communication lines from each remote site to the service center database will need to be in place. The application software, however, is key to developing the two-way integration approach for the shared-service center. Both the properties, as well as the shared-service center, need to invest in software that is capable of replicating data content.

Pros and Cons - Shared Services Model

The two-way, integrated shared—services model is geared towards repetitive transactions that can be somewhat automated or handled through mass processing. Companies that have numerous locations that handle the same types of transactions can also realise significant savings. The shared-service model, however, requires major upfront investment in new technologies, as well as commitment to planning and organisational change processes. Developed in-house, costs can range from new hardware and software purchases to relocation costs of employees leaving their location to work in the service center.

The initial investment in the service center includes application hardware and software expense, the WAN and LAN costs, rent and building improvements, employee relocation and severance expense, initial training and change management expenses, and the costs to implement the new structure. The on-going costs include the training and procedure development, communication costs, payroll and other overhead expenses.

Scenario Two

Setting

A hotel management company manages 40 properties in different locations. Each property has varying technological infrastructures handling its data, but corporate management is seeking to combine property purchases to realise significant vendor discounts through volume purchasing.

Scenario

A large wine distributor delivers the corporate-approved

house wine to one property in California, while another wine distributor delivers the same corporate-approved house wine to another property in Washington state.

Problem

Different volume purchases have to be made to distinct properties by different distributors, but the original price negotiated with the producer (winery) remains the same. This becomes an accounting and reporting issue for each property to insure that each purchase is billed at the corporate negotiated price. Again, since financial reporting can be very slow, it may be days before the bill is verified with the accounts payable and purchase order to show the correct account balance.

Two-way integration Solution

The solution to this scenario lies in the design of the shared-service center, and the functionality of its finance and accounting system. The property purchasing system and the corporate or shared-service system need to be aligned with each other to update the data on a regular and accurate basis. Using a two-way interface solution, the properties and corporate can view the correct price and total volume of purchases throughout the system at any point in time.

The Hybrid Integration - "Complexing" Approach

A third option is a hybrid of the Superbase and shared-service center approaches. Using a clustering or complexing structure within a confined geographical boundary, an organisation can enjoy some of the benefits of the two-way integration approach for a select number of properties, but without some of the costs associated with developing a shared-service center.

Using a WAN, this method processes information or transactions at one site/property for multi-properties in the local geographic region. What distinguishes this approach from the one-way Superbase method is the assumption that the combining properties use the same technology and business rules at the property' level. This can sometimes be found in a particular region or city where properties of a similar brand are standardised in their informational reporting and technology specifications.

Pros and Cons of the Hybrid Approach

This method benefits organisations that adopt a regional management structure. By linking a few properties to a central site, the organisation receives some of the two-way integration advantages without spending the requisite costs to develop a shared-service center. In addition, overhead and communication costs can be kept low while reducing some headcount. As supporting documentation can be kept within reach, operators can also receive the added benefit of knowing that back-up files and information is easily accessible.

The drawbacks to the hybrid approach depend on the level of technology existing in the clustering of properties. If each property has its own proprietary systems, the cost for a hybrid solution may be more than the one-way Superbase approach. In addition, the regional structure does little to contribute to the enterprise solution the organisation still has the issue of consolidating multi-property information in an integrated fashion.

The Right Approach

The best integration approach depends not only on your organisation's strategic goals and objectives, but also the level of functionality and investment that is required to provide high guest value in a multi-property environment.

While a shared-service center approach might be suitable for a highly centralised company with properties distributed across a wide geographic region, a one-way Superbase approach may be more applicable to a decentralised company that requires enterprise-level data in limited and time-independent increments.

Prior to a merger, consideration should be given to the level of technology resident in each respective entity. An operational due diligence in a merger should include a broad understanding of the target company's processes, technology (property management, gaming, sales, POS, ERP, HR, and central reservation systems) and back office facilities (i.e. accounting). When considering integration options in a newly formed merged or multi-property environment, it is important to assess the future information needs of the organisation and determine whether your company is best suited to provide it.

If the information that you are seeking to provide has limited differentiation in the eyes of the customer with no enduring competitive advantage, then perhaps the activity should be outsourced. Ultimately, only those market leaders who "stick to their knitting" and focus on their core competitive strengths will deliver on the promise of greater efficiency in a multi-property environment.

9

Public Market Financing of the Hospitality Industry

Securitisation of hotel property and corporate financing has been a popular item in capital markets in the United States during the last several years and looks set to become a permanent feature on the financing landscape. Elsewhere around the world, the use of public markets to fund the international hotel industry is spotty at best. For many years, the U.S. hotel industry benefited from the largesse of private institutional capital, primarily the insurance industry, savings institutions and commercial banks to fund property expansion and acquisition. With these resources no longer as available, the industry has been forced to turn to alternative sources such as the public market and has had to adjust to a new set of rules.

REITs

In US, Real Estate Investment Trusts or REITs (which distribute earnings from real estate, free of corporate taxes) had become high fliers in the stock market. Having finally dealt with the structuring challenges that are unique to REITs and previously made hotel REIT formations problematic, a series of issues came to market in late 1993.

These tended to be relatively small issues but they delivered some of the best stock performance in the REIT sector, with investor interest driven largely by the turnaround in the U.S. hotel industry that continues to this day.

Following these initial successes, secondary offerings came to market during 1994 and the general enthusiasm was palpable. But with interest rate escalations throughout the year, the fervor began to fade and by late 1994, the market had retreated. Uncertainty concerning the outlook for hotel REITs was widespread with the conventional wisdom being that it would be a while before we would see any resurgence of interest. Well, what a difference a year can make.

There was a renewed interest in REITs late in 1995 signaled by the successful launch of the largest hotel REIT yet—the $305 million Patriot American issue involving a portfolio of 20 hotels. And earlier in the year, Starwood Capital successfully recapitalised Hotel Investors Trust, a "grandfathered" REIT that had been operating for years with a unique paired share structure that allows the REIT to manage as well as own property—something other REITs are not allowed to do. As these large hotel REITs have come to market, there appears to be an appreciation for size that translates into more favorable pricing. This suggests that small capitalisation REITs may not see as much popularity as heretofore when they essentially had the market to themselves.

REITs both large and small are but examples, however, in a large public financial marketplace that is increasingly serving the capital needs of the U.S. hotel industry. During the last four years, approximately $4 billion of capital has been raised for publicly traded hotel companies and $1 billion for hotel REITs—split evenly between debt and equity. And the pace quickened in 1995 with a steadily rising stock market.

Hotel industry financings were up by one-third over the prior year at approximately $2 billion. Following the fall-off in the REIT market late in 1994, the market for new hotel REITs had been slow in returning. But with the success of the large Patriot American deal, the market seems ready for more. Easier to predict than volume is the style or structure of future hotel REIT financings. Hotel REITs have also tended to be all equity offerings with lines of credit to fund expansion—but these lines can run out quickly following an active property acquisition programme.

Future hotel REITs will therefore need to develop capital structures that present blends of debt and equity in an effort to reduce the weighted cost of capital and provide for better balance as the capital base is expanded. Since quality sponsorship is so critical to success in public markets, it also appears likely that we will see fewer Initial Public Offerings (especially during a period of consolidation) and more secondary offerings involving the return to market of well-established hotel companies with a proven track record. No matter how much enthusiasm exists for the industry's positive economic situation, there is little doubt the focus in the future will be on management and its ability to deliver through the next cycle.

In addition to the return of hotel REITs last year, there was also a resurgence of activity involving "C" Corporations - traditionally structured companies that have historically been the main players in the public market, A series of new C-corp issues attracted a great deal of institutional investor interest, something that is not always as prevalent on the REIT side of the market.

Some small C- corp issues also showed very strong growth stories as the hotel market has turned around. This has attracted a lot of new investors, which is clearly healthy in broadening the base of investor support for the industry. An interesting trend is the growing acceptance of hotel real estate as part of a public company's balance sheet. Notwithstanding the tendency for the stock market to focus on short-term earnings, some of the recent hotel C corp issues have suggested that hotel property ownership can be appreciated, particularly if it delivers operating leverage in a period of rising occupancy. Of course this appreciation can disappear quickly in a downturn when the leverage works in reverse and delivers losses very quickly.

The public market tends to value a growth story. Working against this concept in the REIT arena is the requirement of the tax code that 95 percent of a REIT's earnings be distributed out to the investors each year. As a consequence, for those companies trying to build franchise value through customer relationships and in need of a constant source of reinvestment capital, the REIT structure is not generally a suitable vehicle. But for those with large real estate portfolios, judicious use of the REIT format for "off balance sheet" property financing can produce a satisfactory outcome.

The lease format used by hotel REITs to address the tax laws' prohibition of involvement in the management of the property, tends to secure a long-term involvement with the property—something that is of particular value in a market where traditional property owner/manager relationships have become far more tenuous and unpredictable. In the context of the hospitality industry at large, it is worth mentioning the gaming industry's involvement with public market financing. Gaming companies have long been involved with the public markets as a result of not being able to tap into private institutional sources of money.

Without the respectability that it has today, gaming companies originally had to operate in the high-yield market. And as the gaming sector grew and the earnings escalated with new jurisdictions, a compelling story for gaming stocks has developed in recent years. More recently we have seen the setbacks of poor press, some negative votes against new jurisdictions and one or two high-profile bankruptcies. This can quickly dampen the enthusiasm, and so it remains to be seen as to what the longer-term public market environment will be like for gaming companies.

For those with experienced management, a well established franchise and customer following, and a position in established jurisdictions, there should be few difficulties. For those at the margin, however, it will be another story. And indeed we can expect to see a consolidation and shakeout as the gaming industry refocuses its attention on the strong players who are well-positioned to benefit from the trends in a variety of gaming jurisdictions across the country.

The countervailing view is that public market investors driven by the hype surrounding a bull market may value a high-profile hospitality company significantly in excess of what the private market might judge the stock to be worth - the herd mentality one might say. Timing is, of course, everything. As Wall Street becomes more involved in hotel property financing, it is not surprising that the rating agencies have begun to play a role. Ratings have tended to be associated with the packaging of small hotel mortgages into Real Estate Mortgage Investment Conduits or "REMICs." Such conduits tranche the capital into various risk levels that carry a range of ratings and are priced accordingly. REMICs were expected to play a big role in hotel financing especially as these programmes were supported by some of the country's largest franchisors as a service to their franchisees. But they turned out to be relatively expensive for borrowers of small amounts.

As the industry turned around, there was more competition from local banks willing to finally take a closer look at their neighbourhood borrowers who had been ignored since the real estate collapse in 1991. As the rating agencies look at hotel debt issues, the factors of importance include portfolio diversification (both geographic and by property type), the adequacy of management fees, the presence of satisfactory replacement reserves and the structure. Whether rating agencies can play a role in encouraging an expanded role for public market financing of the hotel sector remains to be seen. The early signs are that they are interested in understanding the business and appear willing to participate.

And yet even if there is a willingness on the part of the rating agency community to play a role, it must be recognised that at its heart, the public market is far more fickle than the private market. Sentiments of sup port and enthusiasm for an industry can evaporate quickly if there are unexpected setbacks. Conventional wisdom at the moment, however, seems to suggest that the U.S. hotel industry's fundamentals are positive and the upward trend in profitability should continue for at least two more years.

Demand for hotel rooms, however, tracks extremely closely with the underlying change in Gross Domestic Product. So as goes the economy, thus will follow the hotel industry. And if the economy falters, expect to see some major interruption in the otherwise rosy outlook for hotel stocks and debt issues. But even if the industry continues on its present positive track, we should not assume that the public markets will provide all of the answers to the liquidity crisis for the industry.

Considering the overall size of hotel financing needs in the United States, which we estimate at $8 billion annually, the public markets account for only a modest portion of the need at approximately 15 percent. Because of the hotel industry's fragmented structure, its real estate orientation and its general reputation as part real estate/ part business, we have not seen as many publicly quoted hotel companies as one might expect in an industry of its size. This hopefully will change in future years as the hospitality industry gains further respectability and hotel corporations enlarged through the process of consolidation seek broader access to public capital.

Consolidation can also have a counterpoint, however, and in the U.S. hotel and gaming industries this means de-consolidation. Marriott Corporation split for different reasons in an attempt to separate their real estate from their operational activities. And finally Sheraton Hotels, a stalwart of the U.S. hospitality scene, is now part of a split-up by parent ITT of its varied businesses into three groupings. The first, ITT Destinations, is the consolidation of its hospitality, gaming, sports and entertainment businesses. The public market reactions to these reconstitutions of hospitality companies have by-and-large been favorable, suggesting that it pays to continuously look "outside the organisational box" when trying to create shareholder value.

As hotel groups become larger and operate on a truly global basis, we are likely to see simultaneous hotel company listings in key financial markets around the world such as New York, London and Tokyo, one of the advantages of such international public market exposure relates to the quest that many hospitality companies have for global brand presence. Customer focus deriving from a brand strategy can quite reasonably tie into shareholder relationships on a global scale. It is just a matter of time.

In the past, many lenders and institutional and individual investors have viewed the hospitality industry somewhat suspiciously, and have preferred to provide corporate debt to hotel companies or to purchase shares in quoted hotel companies to spread sector risk as widely as possible. This preference has meant that the industry has been characterised by relatively unsophisticated financings. The ownership structure of the industry in the United Kingdom has also been of influence in this regard.

Hotels tend to be owner-operated and, with relatively few exceptions, the major hotel owning and operating companies are subsidiaries of conglomerates. Where capital has been required for development and M&A activity at such companies, it has normally been provided by the parent company since, generally speaking, corporate debt at such a level is rather less expensive than project or deal-specific debt. Furthermore, in the United Kingdom there are relatively few independent hotel management companies operating hotels under franchises from the major international brands.

In the United States such independent companies have been great users of public market capital. Those which do exist in the United Kingdom are small—in most instances operating two or three hotels. Development and acquisitions activity at such companies tend to be financed on a project-by-project basis with security provided by the asset to be financed plus, in many cases, additional company or personal guarantees. The one major exception to this general rule is the Whitbread Hotel Group, which owns and operates 13 hotels under franchise agreements with Marriott International. Whitbread Hotels Group, however, is a relatively small subsidiary of Whitbread PLC the brewing company, and funds for the £185 million acquisition of the 13 Scott's hotels were provided by the parent company.

Special share issues (such as rights issues and convertible preference share issues), however, have been used among the relatively few quoted "pure" hotel companies—particularly during the late 1980s. Oueen's Moat Houses financed a series of corporate and individual hotel property acquisitions via rights issues. Turning to the future in the United Kingdom, given the capital intensive nature of the industry, we have observed an increasing interest among both the major conglomerates and the independent hotel owned management companies in innovative financing methods—particularly in off-balance sheet financing.

The hospitality sector has been traditionally housed in large corporations with financing obscured from public view. And in Germany, the hospitality industry's experience with the public markets is in its developmental stages, reports Hospitality Consulting Director John Litzenberger of Arthur Andersen's Frankfurt office. Kempinski is the only publicly quoted company with just six hotels in Germany and a total portfolio of only 30 properties. With an overbuilt domestic market, there is little demand for new capital, public or otherwise to fund new activities.

The large German chains are by-and-large privately owned—Maritim, Steigenberger and Arabella—and do not come to the public market for capital. Closed-end property funds that do trade publicly will have some exposure to hotel real estate but it tends to be mixed into a large diversified portfolio. In Australia, Phil Kasselis, Director of Hospitality Consulting in the firm's Sydney office, reports that the Australian Stock Exchange has 16 listed companies in a Tourism and Leisure Index.

The TL Index was established in 1994 with over half the index made up of casino stocks. The index outperformed the market by a factor of 3:1 in 1995, confirming the enthusiasm investors have for the fast developing gaming industry and the fundamentals of the hotel sector, where demand growth continues to outstrip supply and should continue to do so for the next several years and probably up to the year 2000 when Sydney hosts the Olympics.

In the Australian property funds, where hotels as an asset class are generally under-represented, we should see an increase in the allocation of capital to this sector as profits return and the hotel industry outlook remains positive. Casino operators, hotel owners and hotel management companies will also expand their presence in the public financial markets, finding it a cheaper and easier way to raise capital than traditional bank debt. Large institutions are also likely to increase their involvement with publicly listed hospitality companies.

In short, the international hotel industry has a long way to go in truly capitalising on the opportunities afforded by public financial markets. The securitisation of real estate has developed rapidly in recent years in the United States, but may be much longer in coming to other markets elsewhere, where traditional methods of financing are slow to change.

Financial adversity will, however, force users of capital to source their needs in the public domain. It will require some big adjustments in approach and some serious corporate soul searching to get there. But it can be worth it and in a world of capital shortage, hospitality companies may have no choice but to force their way in. And as they say in the travel business... getting there is half the fun.

10

From Physical Assets to Customer Equity

The hospitality industry has historically measured itself with a standard metric used worldwide—revenue-per-available-room (REVPAR). More than simply a way to quantify results, REVPAR reflects our industry's fundamental structure and value proposition based on physical assets (hotel rooms) as the driver of wealth. With the magnitude of change driven by technology, it is now essential to ask is REVPAR still the best measure of performance for a hotel organisation, or does it reflect an outmoded view of a hotel's performance horizon?

Technology is changing every aspect of how we live, work and profit, and it should come as no surprise that technology must also change how the hospitality industry serves customers and measures itself. In short, the "end game" can no longer be REVPAR—revenue measured by the physical asset. The most profitable hotel organisations of the future will be those that capture an increasing share of the customer's purchasing power—while they are in the hotel, at home or anywhere else in the world. What drives this change is technology, which makes it possible to serve customers in both physical place (the hotel room) and virtual space.

The historic measure of hotel performance—REVPAR—must thus give way to a metric that reflects the customer as the more fundamental driver of value in the hospitality industry. Revenue-per-available-customer (REVPAC) does just that. In our contemporary world, hotel organisations are no longer constrained by physical location in serving customers. New media and systems technologies offer extraordinary efficiencies in delivering products and services with greater speed, lower cost and improved flexibility.

Furthermore, technology offers unprecedented opportunities for innovation in an industry's changing menu of products and services. We are witnessing a period of major change as the fundamental value proposition of our industry is overturned. Customers—not physical assets—drive wealth in all industries, and the hospitality industry is certainly no exception. Technology deployed in enterprise-wide platforms makes it possible to get closer to customers. It provides tangible benefits as it offers opportunities to increase business value, reduce operational costs and create new opportunities for growth in the industry.

CUSTOMER EQUITY

At stake is technology's impact on customer equity - defined as the degree to which an industry has fully developed relationships with its customers, providing them with more products and services to meet exiting and emerging needs. REVPAC, as a measure of performance, embodies a shift in perspective from an "asset play" based on hotel properties and rooms to a focus on leveraging customer equity for shareholder wealth.

REVPAC casts a spotlight on a number of key questions for the industry on the eve of the 21st century. How can hotel organisations "talk" to customers in a way they have never been spoken to before by the industry? What must companies do to "hear" their customers in new ways, learning how to better represent them and their needs in the market? How can hospitality organisations maximise revenues by making the most of their relationships with customers? Hotel guests are not lust customers who seek room and board, and perhaps a fax machine in the room. They represent a consumer with an array of needs, whose time is Limited and who, in many cases, will respond to diverse products, improved service and convenience.

In the future, the traditional "marketplace" (the physical realm made up of destinations and hotel buildings) will be greatly expanded to incorporate the virtual environment or "marketspace" - a market context and environment rendered accessible by technology as physical location becomes irrelevant. Understanding the potential of both the marketplace and marketspace sets the stage for delivery of expanded products and services - some traditional, others less so - to customers.

Technology thus plays a key role, both in delivering products and service in virtual space, but also in enhancing the ability to listen and talk with customers in new ways. Sophisticated management information systems allow companies to identify with increasing precision the customer segments and markets that offer the greatest opportunities for growth, given the pace of change in a global economy. A technology platform must incorporate two systems, however, to support the hospitality industry's potential for improving customer equity.

Customer reservations systems track when and where customers are going, and what they will do when they get there. Customer information systems track who the customers are, what they purchase, and how they live and work. Hospitality companies already use reservation systems to get customers into the hotel. Information systems generate customer profiles based on tracking consumption patterns in the process defining a diverse range of wants and needs.

This poses a number of challenges. Certainly, it will be important to integrate data generated at the property level with reservations systems and customer information in a total system solution that provides for data warehouses and networked communications. In such a system, customer information is captured from a variety of sources, and becomes the platform for the highly focused marketing and product development strategies of the future.

The hospitality in the industry will thus require two types of infrastructure to do business—real estate and technology—to support a shirt from depending on "place" to a reliance on "space" to fully meet customer needs. This follows a four-stage evolution currently taking place in industries across the board.

The hospitality industry, for example, historically focused on developing major physical assets, with an almost exclusive orientation to financing and building individual properties. At this first stage, companies achieved relatively low customer equity, providing a narrow band of products and services, traditional to the hospitality industry, at various physical locations. As the industry matured, it differentiated itself to meet more diverse customer needs with properties matched to the various market niches. In this second stage, business hotels and all-suite properties are examples of such differentiation. A third stage involves serving customers in ways that do not require a physical address at all, including telephone marketing and catalogue sales. And in the fourth state—the age of electronic commerce - the "real estate" is actually owned by the consumers themselves in the form of a personal computer located on a desktop, eliminating the need for many types of businesses to own significant physical assets in order to create wealth.

At each of these stages, the potential for customer equity rises with increased access to customers, regardless of their physical location, while the costs associated with fixed-assets (real estate) declines. The evolutionary track moves from exclusive reliance on major assets to combinations of physical assets and technology in reaching customers. Indeed, new media and systems technologies can be designed to give hotel organisations greatly enhanced access to larger numbers of customers—regardless of physical location. These technology platforms also spawn rapid innovation in products and services, combined with improved speed to market. The result enhanced business valuation and higher stock prices as a company's strategic, technological and financial architectures are aligned to generate customer equity.

Hospitality companies can dramatically improve the valuation of their companies by using new technology to bring them closer to their customers. This is particularly the case with major companies that have not fully served their large customer bases and have good potential to build customer equity. In many cases these organisations are our industry's major franchisors, whose goals are typically to sign up new franchisees and improve the yields from each property. In a nutshell, these companies are using franchising as a growth vehicle and their orientation is to maximising fee income.

For these organisations, an intermediate performance measure might be described as revenue-per-available-franchisee (REVPAF). The challenge here will be to develop ways to reach the primary customer (hotel guest) directly, rather than simply through the franchisee organisations—with the end game being improved REVPAC. The typical franchisor catches the primary customer in its reservation system, but typically doesn't "speak" to that customer again, either during the guest stay or after leaving the hotel property. Franchisors will benefit as they begin to develop the strategies and systems allowing them direct access to the primary customers, with a goal of increasing REVPAC.

11

Service Quality in the Hospitality Profession

Generally services are intangible or at least much less tangible than physical goods or products. This lack of possession means that services generally cannot be owned in the same way that manufactured goods can, they can only be experienced, created or participated in, with the result that customers may find it difficult to evaluate the services rendered.

Essentially, 'pure' services are more concerned with a performance rather than an object and unsurprisingly this has engendered the use of theatrical metaphors to characterise service work, an example being Disney's wellknown use of 'back-stage' and 'on-stage'. Experts suggest that often the lack of a tangible product makes it difficult for service organisations to differentiate themselves 'since customers do not always understand what information is being conveyed by different competitors.' In response to such problems they suggest that service companies may seek to 'tangiblise' the intangible via such things as standardising the exterior and interior of buildings to create an image which customers will immediately recognise, a strategy pursued with considerable success by companies such as McDonald's.

Hardware can be broadly co
physical product (for example, the inte
a hotel, its rooms, meals, beverages an
The software consists of the more amo
service quality, service delivery and
interaction between the producer and con
could be suggested that both the hardw d the software comprise the overall product and in the normative view held by much of the services marketing and management literature must successfully coalesce to ensure organisational success.

Nonetheless, it is widely recognised that within the notion of intangibility, service organisations which offer a product that is, 'intangible dominant', increasingly seek to differentiate themselves on the basis of the software aspects such as seeking high quality and 'authentic' service interactions for the increasingly discerning customer. The key feature of inseparability is the high level of face-to-face or voice-to-voice interaction between buyer (that is, the customer) and seller resultant from the simultaneous production and consumption within the service process. This process has been variously described in hyperbolic terms as the so-called 'Moment of Truth'.

Indeed, this dramaturgical view of service suggests that the organisation, via its front line staff, has to 'get it right first time' in order to ensure a flawless performance which will result in the customer returning to any given service business. More measured and less prescriptive accounts of the service encounter are concerned to recognise a number of elements which pose a range of issues for organisations. This is particularly so on the issue of quality assurance where 'the consumer finds it difficult to isolate service quality from the quality of the service provider'.

Organisations, then, may face significant problems in attempting to manage and control interaction between

..r front line employees and customers. These problems are given a particular focus when we recognise the notion of heterogeneity. Heterogeneity refers to possible variations in service quality due to the labour intensity of most service production, such that 'the quality and essence of a service can vary from producer to producer, from customer to customer, and from day to day'. As a result of this possible variance in employee-customer interactions, service organisations may face difficulties in ensuring uniform quality of service between outlets, especially in branded services.

One of the ways in which organisations have sought to resolve this problem is to reduce the human element in service production by the use of mechanisms such as Automatic Teller Machines in banking for example. An alternative to this approach is to 'industrialise' services, by breaking down service operations into minute and discrete simple tasks to enable semi- and unskilled front line staff to follow a routinised, simple, standardised and often scripted approach to each service encounter, typified by fast food outlets such as McDonald's. This approach has engendered a wide literature which can broadly be seen as polarising between those who see this paradigm as one to be admired and copied or those who excoriate its dehumanising effects.

Increasingly, in addressing this problem of heterogeneity, a key strategy adopted by many service organisations is extensive employee training and development. This involves organisations recognising and acting upon the idea of front line staff being crucial to organisational success and, as a result, supporting things like 'soft' HRM, internal marketing, total quality management (TQM) and empowerment.

Challenge of Service Quality Evaluation

Service quality is more complex to evaluate than in the

case of goods. Services are more difficult to measure and standardise and consequently establishing an instrument attempting to measure quality has become a central challenge for the delivery of good service quality and service companies' success. The challenge of evaluating service quality has been motivated by recent research which increasingly demonstrates the significance of service quality as a central factor of business success. Service quality has consequently become a focus of any management and marketing strategy and high levels of service are seen as a means for organisations to achieve a competitive advantage and position themselves more effectively in the market place.

Customers are also becoming more aware and critical of the alternatives on offer and rising standards of services, prompted by competitive trends, have increased customer expectations. However, service quality may well be increasingly critical to competitive success, 'defining what exactly is "service quality" is somewhat problematic'. Generally service quality cannot be objectively measured as can technical quality for manufactured goods and it therefore remains an elusive and abstract construct.

The characteristics of intangibility, heterogeneity and inseparability presented earlier also constitute a challenge for managers because they do not allow for an easy process of quality evaluation. More importantly, a customer judgement of a service depends as much on the service process as on the outcome, therefore customers' quality evaluation can be seen as depending on the production of services as well as on their consumption. The services marketing and management field has displayed different views of how this construct might be assessed.

For example, Akehurst and Harrington in a review of managerial perceptions of service quality in UK hotels note two schools of thought—American and Nordic—which have sought to address this issue. Though they differ in the detail of their approach, both schools of thought largely adopt a common approach in seeking to group a range of quality items into dimensions.

Quality Dimensionality

Some of the researchers offer an important distinction in their identification of process quality, which is judged by consumers during a service, from output quality, evaluated after a service has been performed. These authors also distinguished between the physical quality, relating to the physical supports of the service, corporate quality, which involves the company's image and profile, and finally interactive quality, which refers to the interactions between a consumer, the service organisation and other customers.

Another type of model proposed a division of service quality into four dimensions: technical quality, integrative quality (the ease with which different portions of the service delivery system work together), functional quality and outcome quality. Other work identified that service quality could be distinguished in two main dimensions, functional and technical quality. Arguably though, the seminal work on quality measurement in services is the SERVQUAL scale, emanated from the American school of thought and aimed to develop a quality scale that would be applicable across different services. The five dimensions were named and described as:

— *Tangibles*: The appearance of physical facilities, equipment, personnel and communication materials.

— *Reliability*: The ability to perform the promised service dependably and accurately.

— *Responsiveness*: The willingness to help consumers and provide prompt service.

— *Assurance*: The knowledge and courtesy of employees and their ability to convey trust and confidence.
— *Empathy*: The caring, individualised attention provided to the customers.

Each of the dimensions contained four to six statement sets. The intent of the statement set was to provide a score for components of the dimension that could also be averaged to provide an overall score of the dimension. Each statement had a corresponding perceived quality score calculated by subtracting the perception score from the expectation score. As a result of a important research effort that this scale demanded, and because of its innovativeness and the contentious issues it raised, the scale has suffered various criticism.

The goal was to produce a generic scale which would translate consumers' quality judgement in any service setting: The instrument has been designed to be applicable across a broad spectrum of services. As such, it provides a basic skeleton through its expectations/perceptions format encompassing statements for each of the five dimensions. The skeleton, when necessary, can be adapted or supplemented to fit the characteristics or specific research needs of a particular organisation.

However, further replications of the scale to different types of services have clearly demonstrated that its pre-supposed universal nature was refutable. This does not necessarily mean that the scale should be rejected completely but rather that consideration should be given to its suitability to specific services and its necessary adaptation to new service contexts.

Hospitality has been a fertile ground for research with numerous different applications of SERVQUAL. Some of the analysis shows that the first dimension explains most of the variance observed therefore giving poor credibility to the four other dimensions and the multidimensionality of the service quality construct. Another study on hotels provided different findings from the previous application, and the reproduction of the SERVQUAL dimensions were not confirmed either. Researchers followed step by step the SERVQUAL methodology and created a new scale, named LODGSERV, which displayed only three dimensions: tangibility, reliability and contact.

To add to the confusion compared the SERVQUAL and LODGSERV scales and concluded that 'both scales fail to replicate the proposed dimensions and to provide content validity in this specific application'. Furthermore, another application of SERVQUAL to hotel and motel services identified LODGSERV but this scale simply replicated SERVQUAL to the context studied. The SERVQUAL format commented on high expectations scores observed. Some items were also classified as dissatisfies and were defined as elements which would cause dissatisfaction by their absence but would not influence customers' satisfaction by their presence since customers assume that they would be present.

Lastly, and most recently, surveyed 155 three to five star hotels in Australia using a modified version of the SERVQUAL scale. Survey aimed to test the reliability of the SERVQUAL model by establishing the number of dimensions of service quality in the hospitality industry in an attempt to determine which dimension is the best predictor of overall service quality. The amended version of SERVQUAL added eight items which were considered to specifically pertain to the hospitality industry and deleted three items. This customised version of SERVQUAL was renamed HOLSERV.

Based on this findings there are three dimensions of service quality in hospitality, employees, tangibles and reliability (Table 1) and argue that '...the employees dimension emerged as the best predictor of overall service quality.'

Table 1. Dimensions of service quality in the hospitality industry

Factor	Elements from SERVQUAL	Main emphasis
Employees (factor 1)	Responsiveness Assurance Empathy Tangibles	Prompt service, willingness to help. confident in the delivery of of service, polite, knowledgeable, skilful, caring, understanding sincere, neat and professional employees.
Tangibles (factor 2)	Tangibles	Modern-looking equipment, fixtures and fittings, appealing facilities and materials, comfort, cleanliness, user friendly equipment and facilities, variety in food and beverages, operation of services at a convenient time.
Reliability (factor 4)	Reliability Responsiveness Assurance	Keeping promises, accurate and timely service, safe and secure stay.

Generalisation of SERVQUAL

It is believed that the problems encountered in the limited generalisation of SERVQUAL might be linked to the particularities of the services upon which it was developed. Indeed, the SERVQUAL scale was built from the study of four commercial services, namely repair and maintenance, retail banking, credit card and securities brokerage. These services involve situations in which consumers buy a service for rational and functional purposes. The service delivery usually encompasses a short service encounter principally monitored by an employee and the delivery takes place in a limited environment.

Indeed, most tourism and hospitality services may potentially involve complex processes, multiple encounters and a longer involvement with the service firm. For example, the consumption of a tourist attraction involves contacts with different staff, with a multitude of tangible aspects (the attraction itself, décor, ambience, comfort, objects looked upon, rides) and the evaluation of different services provided (the attraction, restaurant, cafe, shop).

Similarly, consumers using a hotel will come across a multitude of tangible aspects (the hotel, décor, layout of the rooms, atmosphere) and a variety of services (room service, cleaning, catering services, reception, bar, leisure centre). Therefore the encounters are multiple and varied and all need to be integrated in the evaluation processes of service quality. More importantly, these different service features imply that the nature of the service delivery might follow different patterns.

For example, in certain hospitality services the encounter with staff might remain relatively limited and the tangibles aspects might be quite important suggesting that the evaluation processes could be based on different criteria. This recognition of diversity is believed to be at the centre of the SERVQUAL controversy. It is recognised that the potentiality to build a generic scale is unrealistic since it would wrongly suggest that services display similar service delivery features and that customers would use similar criteria to evaluate service quality. In fact, recognition of the limits of SERVQUAL to represent the diversity of services has already been recognised by several authors.

If other services categories had been included (in the SERVQUAL scale), particularly professional services which are high in terms of opportunities for consumer intervention and adaptation, it is possible that other factor groupings would have emerged, possibly associated with one or more of the 'incorporated' dimensions: competence, credibility, security or knowledge for example.

The SERVQUAL authors believed they had built their scale upon services whose 'categories were chosen to represent a broad cross-section of services that varied along key dimensions'. However, SERVQUAL was in fact built on very similar services. Consequently, the SERVQUAL authors' conclusion that the relative importance of the dimensions identified were consistent across service settings, was considered as unrealistic. More importantly, these authors compared the relative importance of the SERVQUAL dimensions across services displaying different degrees of interaction and customisation.

The relative importance of the five SERVQUAL dimensions in four new service contexts: teaching, restaurants, health care and bookstores. The results showed that the reliability dimension always remained the most important predictor of overall satisfaction for all the services investigated. However, services appeared to display different importance ratings for the dimensions according to their characteristics: in high interaction—high customisation services 'knowing the customer' was rated as the most important dimension whereas in low interaction-low customisation services, 'reliability' and 'tangibles' were the first two dimensions. The importance of service quality dimensions would differ according to the service characteristic

Implications

While most of the existing literature examining service quality has focused increasingly heavily on personnel contacts with customers, within certain areas of hospitality, for example hotel services, the tangible elements of the hospitality product are also extremely important. This, in part, is due to the fact that when using those services, consumers will tend to spend a longer period of time within the premises than for other services.

For instance, the tangibles of a bank or a repair company can be assumed to be of lesser importance to consumers because these are not central to the service provision but also because the consumers will spend a relatively shorter period of time within those premises. In the case of hotel services, it can be argued that since consumers will spend a longer period of time, tangibles will become a central part of the product consumption.

Indeed, the notion of product consumption is key here because in a hotel, compared to a bank, as well as the longer temporal dimension customers are also consuming the tangible aspects of the room, restaurant, leisure centre and so on as an integral aspect of the core product. This is less likely to be true in a bank where the tangibles would ordinarily merely provide a meeting place between consumers and producers, they do not represent the product which is being bought and consumed by the customers. A study on the determinants of service quality in airline services indicated that physical dimensions such as food quality or seating comfort were very important factors in service quality evaluations, again this was a service where consumers spend a relatively longer period of time in the physical space.

More importantly, a recent study on hotel services clearly highlighted the specificity of that service context: 'Services differ in the proportions of tangibles they contain. It would be reasonable to suppose that the importance of tangible aspects is higher in customer experiences such as hotel services, which contain a high proportion of clearly differentiated tangible components'.

Whilst hotels can be both labour and capital intensive it is the former which has often generated the greatest interest and initiatives: The modern hotel industry has tended to promote its obsession with customer service delivery standards while ignoring the need for the hotel product to meet the expectations of the customer. Put another way 'soft' human and interactional processes are promoted as the principle means of ensuring customer satisfaction to the extent that attention to the 'hard' elements of the hospitality product is diminished.

Customer expectations have evolved and that evidence points to an increasing interest in the quality of the product rather than the service. Scepticism of the need for organisations to consider the softer aspects of the service encounter, much of the work that has emerged in relation to more prescriptive accounts of service quality have tended to point to the human dimension. Thus, although the tangibles are perceived as being important, the human dimension through the employee service is also particularly relevant. In sum, customer perceptions of quality will vary from service to service and will, at various times, encompass different aspects.

Indeed, in many respects notions of service quality may be as much about consistent delivery to the specified offer, whether high or low specification. As a corollary, this review of the dimensionality of service quality clearly reinforces the notion that the relative importance of quality dimensions will change between a fast food restaurant and Michelin starred restaurant or a basic budget hotel and a deluxe hotel. Equally this also points to the obvious point that differing HRM approaches are likely to be appropriate to differing service settings and it is this issue which is now considered by firstly reflecting upon the relationship generally between competitive strategy and HRM before moving on to the service sector specifically.

Product Market Strategies and HRM

One of the earliest and most influential attempts to develop a model which theorised the relationship between competitive strategy and HRM was that offered by Schuler and Jackson. Building on the earlier seminal work undertaken by Porter on competitive strategy, and particularly routes to gaining competitive advantage, Schuler and Jackson developed a series of typologies of 'needed role behaviours' that enabled the link between competitive strategy and HRM practices to be made.

The type of needed role behaviours within Schuler and Jackson's model was contingent on the overall strategies that an organisation could adopt to seek competitive advantage and the concomitant HRM approached adopted to sustain this. First, there is an innovation strategy, where organisations seek to develop products or services which are different from competitors, such that the focus here is on companies offering something new and different. Organisations adopting this approach seek to develop an environment where innovation is allowed to flourish.

Resultantly, the employee needed role behaviour in such a scenario is characterised by things like a willingness to tolerate ambiguity and unpredictability, the need to be creative and risk taking. Given these characteristics the type of HRM strategy flowing from this approach is based on having a large number of highly skilled individuals who are likely to enjoy high levels of autonomy. Second, is the quality enhancement strategy wherein firms seek to gain competitive advantage by enhancing the product and/or service quality. The approach once again points to certain HRM practices to support a total quality approach. These practices include the encouragement of feedback systems, teamwork, decision making and responsibility being an integral part of an employees job description and flexible job classifications.

The intent of these practices is to create needed employee behaviour such as co-operative, interdependent behaviour, and commitment to the goals of the organisation. Lastly, the cost reduction strategy sees firms attempting to gain competitive advantage by aiming to be the lowest cost producer within a particular market segment. The characteristics of firms seeking to pursue this strategy are tight controls, minimisation of overheads and pursuit of economies of scale, in the pursuit of increased productivity. In following such a strategy organisations may use higher number of part timers, seek to simplify and measure work via narrowly defined jobs that encourage specialisation and efficiency, and offer short-term results oriented appraisal.

Needed employee behaviours include, repetitive and predictable behaviour, low risk taking activity and a high degree of comfort with stability. As Schuler and Jackson freely admit the description of these three competitive strategies as pure types often does not reflect the reality of, for example, organisations pursuing two or more competitive strategies simultaneously. Nevertheless, this work remains useful for its clear delineation of differing approaches to HRM and the concomitant support for a 'best fit' approach to HRM. Although not necessarily explicitly providing the basis for much of the work which has emerged on these questions in the more specific context of the services marketing and management literature, the influence of Schuler and Jackson can clearly be seen.

For example, Bowen, Schneider and Kim note: When a firm competes on low-cost, high-volume service offerings, it needs to question whether there is any value added from spending additional resources on the more complicated selection, training and even higher compensation that might be necessary to support empowerment. If the targeted market segment values inexpensive, speedy service - not TLC - the...production-line approach of procedurally driven, low employee-discretion jobs might be the best fit. Alternatively, if the strategy is to compete on the provision of differentiated,

TLC service, then designing an HRM mix to empower employees might provide customised service to customers would be appropriate.

Clearly Bowen et al. are arguing for the importance of HRM practices 'fitting' the organisations own strategically defined market segment. This support for the need to generate congruence between the three crucial functional areas of marketing, operations and HRM is commonplace in much of the service marketing and management literature. Indeed, in an earlier work Schneider and Bowen warned organisations not to fall into what they term the 'human resources trap', wherein service firms place excess reliance on their employees as a means to customer satisfaction. Even, then, within the more prescriptive work on service management generally there is a clear recognition of the need for a measured reading of the relationship between product market strategies and HRM.

Again, though not explicitly mentioning the work of Schuler and Jackson, Lashley and Taylor's work evidences much the same thinking in their description of four basic archetypes within which hospitality organisations can be potentially located. Having firstly offered the caveat as to the extent to which the strategy making process remains rational and clearly developed by managers, Lashley and Taylor go on to advocate a 'hierarchy of effects' that should flow from the strategic level down and through functional and tactical levels. They further note, 'In simple terms having formulated its basic mission statement, the service organisation would decide upon both its marketing and competitive strategy.'

Lashley and Taylor developed their model by utilising matrices provided by Schmenner and Heskett et al. to identify different processes in service operations management. These processes are the service factory, the service shop, mass service and professional services. These characterisations are based on the degree of customisation and labour intensity involved in the service offer, in terms of the degree of customer contact required between employees and customers.

The service factory is relatively low labour intensity and low customisation, i.e. high standardisation. The service factory is most obviously exemplified by fast food operators, especially McDonald's. The service shop involves more customisation, but relatively low labour intensity. The defining difference to the service factory lies in the degree of standardisation within the process. Lashley and Taylor draw upon the example of TGI Fridays to argue that although there are high levels of standardisation in the tangible aspects of the organisation, such as the menus, layouts, décor and staff uniform, there is also some scope to customise the customers' eating and drinking experience.

This customisation is by virtue of their more extensive menu, and more importantly, greater spontaneity and authenticity in the intangible aspects of the service provided by front-line staff. The next classification is mass service where service processes involve a relatively high degree of labour intensity, though a limited amount of customisation. Lashley and Taylor assert that the Marriott hotel brand typifies a mass service organisation. The rationale for such an assertion lies in the fact that their four star offering is similar to others in relation to the hardware of the tangibles reflecting the highly competitive nature of the mid to upper segment of the hotel market.

As a result of this convergence of the tangibles the key lies in the intangibles and the scope available to organisations to differentiate themselves on the basis of service quality. Within this process of differentiation a key role is played by the staff via the relatively high level of contact with customers. The final grouping is professional services where there is a high level of service to individual customers and a high degree of labour intensity, as exemplified by hospitality management consultants.

Again, the key point which emerges from the work of Lashley and Taylor is the likely relationship between the service operation type adopted by the organisation and the style of HRM which best fits it. For example, it is apparent that in the four star hotel sector a broadly 'soft' approach to HRM—or what Lashley and Taylor term 'the participative style', as exemplified by high discretion in relation to the intangibles, moral involvement and a moderate trust culture—is suggested as being important to sustain a high quality, TQM-based approach to the service offering. At the other end of the spectrum, McDonald's are suggested as exemplifying a command and control style which is characterised by things such as low discretion for employees, limited responsibility and autonomy and scripted service encounters.

Importantly, Lashley and Taylor do not see the command and control approach in a pejorative way and indeed recognise: ...the historic success of the McDonald's organisation in delivering their market offer...is partly due to the ability to develop and maintain a close fit between the key characteristics of the strategic drivers and actual service delivery through utilisation of an appropriate HRM style.

Having discussed at some length the choices potentially available to hospitality organisations in developing product market and HRM strategies the paper now turns to consider the sector in more detail. Consideration of the sector offers some potential answers as to why there may be reliance upon cost based competitive strategies, with low specification goods and the attendant 'poor' HRM practices and lack of skills within the hospitality workforce.

12

Policy Dimensions of Human Resource Management

A "people" focus, within tourism and hospitality, is by no means new and successful organisations such as Disney, British Airways, Singapore Airlines, Marriott and Ritz Carlton have developed strong reputations for their recognition of the role which their staff play in meeting customer expectations within their sector. Best practice, in the area, appears to recognise that quality service delivery is not the outcome of an isolated service enhancement training programme, but has to do with change in organisational culture from top down and is a complex process which impacts on all areas of the organisation and its systems. It is also a process which is rather more commonly taken aboard within the context of larger organisations.

Small to medium-sized enterprises (SMEs), which have the advantage of simple internal communication systems, face other challenges reflective of their resource structures, expertise and nature of their workforce. There is little doubt that consumer experience of "human value added" through service is varied within and between the hospitality sectors of most countries. In part, this is a reflection of the eclectic nature of customer expectations which may demand very different things from the same service delivery situation. It is also a factor of the number of human interactions (moments of truth) which most customers experience within any one hospitality purchase—these may or may not be within the one organisation and thus the ability to "control" the customer's experience may not lie within the organisation, which suffers through lost business. In many respects, a customer's assessment of hospitality will be based on the total destination experience.

Human resource management is more than a strategic and operational concern for companies competing within the hospitality marketplace. It considers human resource management as a strategic dimension within the wider enhancement of quality and market positioning of tourism at the level of organisations, specific destinations, regions within countries or whole nations. The main thesis advanced is that the tourism and hospitality industry, from the perspective of all its stakeholders (public sector, private sector, visitors and host community), benefits from the close integration of human resource, labour market and education policies, with those policies relating to, and impacting on, the tourism and hospitality sector.

Human Resource in Hospitality Environment

The tourism and hospitality sector, in all locations, has a close relationship with the labour market environment from which it draws its skills and consequently depends on its workforce for the delivery of service and product standards to meet existing and anticipated demand from its visitor marketplace.

This relationship is, on the one hand, one of dependency in that the make-up of the local workforce (or that which can be introduced into the local environment) has a direct influence on the standards and character of the tourist offering which can be prepared and presented to visitors—if local art and craft skills are not developed within the education system or at community level, it will not be possible to offer this dimension to visitors. On the other hand, tourism and hospitality, for many communities, provides a major and growing sector of the economy and, with it, employment opportunities which other traditional and declining sectors of the economy may not provide.

This is true in an industrial, urban context where cities such as Glasgow (now the second most visited urban centre in the UK) have developed tourism in the wake of the decline of its traditional heavy industrial sector. It is an equally valid scenario in locations where the exploitation of natural resources no longer provides the same level of employment opportunity as it did in the past—the decline of the North Atlantic fishery has seen island locations, such as the Faroes, Iceland, Greenland and Newfoundland, focus on tourism as part of wider economic diversification strategies.

Here illustrates, the two-way relationship between tourism and hospitality, and human resource development and management is not always recognised in a holistic and policy-focused manner by public or private sector concerns. Issues which literature and practical experience identified as the major human resource concerns faced by tourism and hospitality at both a practical, operational level and in the context of wider strategic and policy-oriented discussion. These were:

Demography and the shrinking employment pool resulting in labour and specific skills shortages. This is primarily a developed country phenomenon found in Western Europe, North America and "tiger economy" countries of the Far East. However, labour shortage is also a concern elsewhere when it is recognised that the specific skills which tourism demands (technical, cultural, communications) may be in short supply within many, less developed destination areas. Demographic and other forms of structural change within the labour market demand responses which take tourism recruitment beyond its traditional youth pool into consideration of mature worker alternatives (those returning to work; seeking a career change; retirees) and this, in turn, has major implications for relative remuneration, working conditions, employment security and related issues.

For many sub-sectors in tourism and hospitality, and in most developed countries, the negative employment image of the sector is a major issue and barrier to the recruitment and retention of quality and well educated employees. Both industry employees and wider society view hotel and catering labour as relatively low status, mainly because of the personal service nature of the work involved.

This poor image is the result of a cocktail of historic and contemporary factors—the origin of hospitality work within domestic service and its consequent associations with servility; links, in some countries, between hospitality employment and colonial legacy; widespread use of expatriate labour in many developing countries, creating the perception that the sector is one offering only limited opportunity for promotion and progression; widespread exposure to work in the sector as a first working experience, resulting in generalised assessment based on limited exposure; and the reality of anti-social working conditions and casualised remuneration.

In some respects, the negatively-held perceptions are not wholly justified by the reality of work for major airlines, international hotel groups, theme parks or within heritage organisations. In other regards, the perceptions are a mirror of the reality of work within an industrial sector dominated by small and medium-sized enterprises

(SMEs) and the impact of irregular demand. The effect of these perceptions is to impose a barrier to employment and employment choice among school and college leavers, parents and career guidance teachers which has been very difficult to counter.

However, the situation, in some developing countries, is rather different in that international tourism offers a high status and secure employment environment when compared to alternatives in both the primary and manufacturing sectors. In some contexts, cultural and traditional perceptions may also militate against the recruitment of the best able and qualified recruits into the tourism and hospitality sector. Religious barriers, for example, may exclude some groups from participation, notably women.

As already indicated, the rewards and benefits structure of the tourism and hospitality industries can act as a barrier to the recruitment and retention of quality employees. This is a concern of particular focus within hospitality but perceptions regarding working conditions, hours and pay extend more generally across the tourism-related service sector. There is a clear and unavoidable reality, within tourism and hospitality, that the demand cycle is anti-social and falls out with "normal" nine-to-five working parameters. Aircraft fly at night, hotel guests expect services at weekends and theme parks reach peak demand during public holidays.

In terms of remuneration, the sector faces challenges in common with other labour-intensive service areas and in many countries has seen pressures for increased productivity alongside deskilling in many areas of work. At a policy level, the sector is influenced greatly by legislative intervention, for example European initiatives with respect to minimum wage levels, duration of the working week and unsociable working times.

Notwithstanding national and sub-sectoral diversity within tourism and hospitality, a combination of reality and perceptions gives an overall negative gloss to the image of many areas of the industry. This acts as a major barrier to the recruitment of quality personnel into work in the area. Many entrants to work in the sector do so with expectations of impermanence—this reflects reality in terms of the demand cycle (seasonality and fluctuations as a result of instability within the business cycle in general) whereby longer-term and sustained opportunities are not available to those who take employment in hotels, as resort couriers or ski instructors.

It is also reflective of short-termism within many tourism and hospitality businesses which may be unwilling to seek long-term commitment in return for reciprocal long-term investment in the recruit. The sector is one of unconstrained access to most of its working positions and one which, therefore, benefits from unrestrained recruitment to most of its positions but, conversely, also suffers because the skills it engenders in its workforce are in considerable demand within other areas of the service economy.

Thus, while entry is open, so is the opportunity to move out elsewhere, both within tourism and hospitality, and to other employment areas. Staff turnover, therefore, can be very high, especially in tight and competitive labour markets, and is a major inhibitor for organisations and destinations seeking to achieve overall enhancement of service and product quality.

A key issue, relating to recruitment, is that of specific skills shortages in key technical and some managerial areas. In part, this is an extension of the concerns addressed above—image, conditions, remuneration—but is also linked to a reluctance, within some industry sectors and businesses, to invest in the skills development of their key personnel. The Irish tourism industry, throughout a period of sustained growth from the mid-1980s onwards, has experienced acute shortages of key technical personnel, particularly chefs, despite levels of national unemployment considerably above the European Union average.

Contrary trends, however, also raise important issues with respect to recruitment and retention. The combined impact of technology and product substitution in the workplace; centralisation of key management functions (finance, information analysis, marketing); standardisation of product and service delivery; and delayering of management structures in many developed tourism economies means that opportunities for meaningful and developmental careers in skilled craft or managerial areas have been reduced. Reduced opportunity, in turn, impacts on perceptions of the sector and the likelihood of young people, in particular, opting for tourism/hospitality as their career choice.

A changing tourism and hospitality industry environment is, in a sense, complemented but also complicated by changing social expectations of work and an increasingly diverse profile of employees. Diversity provides the opportunity to create new working environments and conditions, but demands comprehensive review of traditional practice. A good example of this is the present reluctance of many employees to accept split-shift working and the consequent need for employers to reorganise their work environment accordingly.

Education, training and development, for tourism and hospitality is also, in part, a recruitment issue in that providers of educational and training programmes, particularly within the college and university sector, are influenced by the same perceptual factors as the industry itself. Recruitment standards to vocational programmes for the sector are lower than those to equivalent courses in related professional areas, for example business. Tourism studies are, in a sense, somewhat different from hospitality in this respect in that vocational outcomes are less clearly defined and graduate choice is likely to be rather more eclectic.

There are clear opportunities to use such educational programmes in a rather more general education sense rather than facing clear vocational channelling. One key issue is a lack of tourism sector consensus as to the need for sector-specific educational provision. Commitment to ongoing career development of existing employees, within tourism and hospitality, varies greatly and is influenced by the sub-sector and the size of the enterprise. The presence of career development opportunities, however, is likely to exert a considerable influence on the retention of ambitious employees, with potential, within the sector.

Recognition remains relatively limited that human resource development is an important contributor to the delivery of quality products and service, within tourism and hospitality, and that this, in turn, impacts on the level of both new and repeat business achieved by businesses and destinations. This situation has altered significantly in recent years and the business advantage achieved, through a people focus, by companies such as British Airways, Singapore Airlines, Marriott and Ritz Carlton, has been an important contributory factor.

However, many small businesses do not have the resources or skills to focus on their human capital. Given that tourism destinations have images that are only as strong as their weakest link, it is important to strive to ensure that the visitor's experience is positive throughout the full range of contact with the providers of goods and services. Human resource development is, frequently, addressed as a reactive concern within tourism and hospitality, and rarely in a proactive and planned sense.

Product and market shifts and developments may be the target of strategic analysis and preparation, but it is not common, within the sector, to find enterprises or wider destination communities putting in place recruitment, education and training in support of such change, whether quantitative or qualitative in advance. Recognition of the lead-time needed to achieve benefit from human resource investment is also limited at both corporate and national levels.

Policy Dimensions of Hospitality

At a practical level, tourism education, training and development within the firm and beyond as part of public or private institutional provision, is relatively mature in most developed countries and is an evolving area of activity to communities and countries for which tourism and hospitality activity is rather more new. There is, however, ongoing and, at times, acrimonious debate between providers of tourism and hospitality education and those who see themselves as clients of the system, the industry itself, regarding the relevance, level and focus of education and training.

One of the difficulties for tourism and hospitality education is that it is expected to dance to the tune of a fragmented and heterogeneous sector where there are few commonly defined needs at a technical or knowledge level. The requirements of major airlines, hotel companies or heritage sites are diverse in themselves but are also significantly different from the needs of SMEs across the sector. The sector also draws in players from areas of activity which may, at best, acknowledge a tenuous association with tourism and hospitality and, at worst, fail to see their responsibilities in this area at all—such areas can include national parks, leisure and recreational interests, the finance sector, the security services and parts of the retail sector.

One of the consequences of a fragmented public and private sector interest in tourism and hospitality is that there is rarely a clear, single authority with responsibility for the management and direction of education, training and development initiatives in support of the sector. In reality, there is frequently a range of organisations and agencies which have some involvement but also have loyalties and interests which lie out with the domain of tourism and hospitality. Such organisations and providers may include:

— the various industry sub-sectors and their representative associations;
— national, regional or local tourism development agencies, generally public but also in the private domain;
— public sector agencies or government authorities responsible for areas such as heritage, the environment, marine and other water resources, agriculture, national parks, etc.;
— national or provincial education providers;
— private education providers;
— specialist training agencies, public and private;
— national employment, labour or manpower agencies and their respective government departments;
— social partner organisations such as trade unions.

What is frequently seen as a practical issue, in that education providers may or may not be delivering appropriate curricula to meet industry's needs, is also an issue of policy concern and, in many respects, it is policy shifts that will be required to provide the lead, and assist the sector and the wider community to face up to predicted changes within tourism and hospitality in the future.

13

Hospitality Industry in the Age of Globalisation

Hotel and travel companies have traditionally viewed technology as an enabler. Large-scale technology implementations have generally been part of efforts to design more robust business processes to reduce costs, improve quality and speed time to market. Once the opportunities are identified, teams assess the role that information technology might play in the implementation. In contrast, Internet technologies are more than enablers in the new economy. They are the drivers of entirely new business models.

The successful companies of the 20th century are beginning to understand that the marketplace of the 21st century requires them to acquire and retain a critical mass of valued customers, and they are developing new competencies to deliver new sources of value to these customers. The foundation of success increasingly is the ability to create new business models that leverage Internet technologies to deliver unique value to customers.

Business to Consumer (B2C)

Diverse factors are driving the successful 20th century

businesses in hospitality and travel to reinvent themselves for the 21st century using eBusiness. But the drivers of change differ in Business to Consumer (B2C) and Business-to-Business (B2B) spaces. In the B2C arena, the desire to strengthen customer relationships, develop new revenue streams, enhance profit margins and create more value are all motivating rapid change. The foundation of success increasingly is the ability to create new business models that leverge Internet technologies to deliver unique value to customers.

The business has moved rapidly and successfully in building high levels of brand awareness out of the starting gate. Loyalty programmes targeting Web-site purchases have now evolved. This new brand awareness and loyalty is a direct threat to the decades of investment in the bricks-and-mortar brands of the industry. As online clearinghouses (businesses selling distressed room inventory) appeal to a growing number of customers, they are directly challenging the hotel brands. The major brand owners have had to fight back. And aligning with competitors in the industry is often perceived to add more value than aligning with the new intermediaries.

Customers' needs do not stay the same. The hotel industry meets the core need of providing a safe and secure home-away-from-home for the business and leisure traveller. But an increasing number of guests—business and leisure, domestic and international - require high-speed Internet access and related capabilities. Guests expect remote-office (and entertainment) environments no less functional than they have at home or in the office.

Incremental Revenue Growth

The new intermediaries have used technology to create other revenue generating tools. There has always been distressed inventory, but networked technologies are allowing the industry to sell it effectively rather than let it perish. There has always been the aspirational non-user of hotel product and services. Now technology is allowing the industry to sell attractively packaged offerings to a market that heretofore has been difficult to identify and reach.

Used intelligently, these businesses are adding a further arrow to the marketer's quiver—enabling the industry to add occupancy by targeting specific (and new) market segments. The extreme last-minute decision-maker and the highly price-sensitive traveller are both in this category. Growing numbers of consumers now compare room facilities and rates, and they are learning to bid for rooms and spare seats on aircraft. A third-party can do the aggregation and the constant updating. It can also act as a brand buffer allowing companies to discount unsold seats or unsold rooms indirectly.

The Internet's cost efficiency appeals to companies that currently manage travel offline, and it should lead to an increase in the number of companies that manage travel overall. We have seen the successful hotel businesses of the old economy partnering to compete with the start-up businesses of the new economy. As these ventures get off the ground, they have the potential to cut deeply into the revenue streams of the new Internet businesses, which have relied on commissions and on the sluggish response to market threats of the airlines and hotel companies.

It will not be that easy to get companies with an ethos of confidentiality to cooperate with competitors—in the process promoting transparency to common customers. But by pooling their resources, the major hospitality and travel chains can develop portals quickly and at lower risk to compete in this dynamically changing market.

The corporate traveller is a key segment targeted by almost all the major brands. Corporate policy, rather than individual choice, increasingly dictates business travel. Corporate policies will increasingly require travellers to use company-approved online booking engines. These engines deliver two elements to improved margins—directed use of a company's negotiated room rates with their preferred suppliers, as well as reduced service charges for making employee travel reservations. Due to the self-service nature of online business travel booking, companies and travel suppliers must increase efforts to encourage continued use.

The Internet's cost efficiency appeals to companies that currently manage travel offline, and it should lead to an increase in the number of companies that manage travel overall. Larger accounts that are currently unmanaged will increasingly buy online and thus will soon adopt managed travel. Even smaller firms will move their business travel online as well, first encouraging individuals to use any Web interface, then gradually adopting targeted services.

Each managed traveller's company computer will include a desktop icon, which, after entering a user name and password, will link directly to a personalised profile within the travel site. Once business travellers sign on to corporate travel sites, entire trips can be booked with one click on the desktop icon, eliminating the need to re-enter login information. On the road, managed travellers will have the ability to research upcoming trips, check on late flights or change an existing hotel reservation.

Due to a combination of new bookers and the increasing amounts consumers are spending, the online travel market continues to boom. Travel sites, however, face the same challenges that online retailers struggle with - most consumers are not loyal. Web travellers rely upon the convenience, abundant information and low prices found online, and they are willing to research multiple sites for the best deals.

Forrester divides customers into three segments: disloyal, curious, and loyal bookers. "Disloyal" bookers, customers who research and book at multiple sites, search far and wide to find the best deals for their sophisticated travel needs—including the lowest prices, enticing special offers and exacting itinerary requirements. "Curious" bookers research multiple sites, yet return to the same site to book travel and accommodations. The third category identified by Forrester, "loyal" customers research and book at one site. Both curious and loyal consumers rely on one site due to easy site navigation, favourable previous experiences and low prices.

B2B Applications

B2B applications are even bigger accelerators of change than those in the B2C space when it comes to how hospitality and travel companies will do business in the years ahead. Even though many customers aggressively seek choices to meet their needs, some sites attract more loyalty than others. The one-stop-shop nature of online travel agencies effectively attracts bookers that rely on one site for all their booking needs. Hotel chains, on the other hand, may have a harder time attracting loyal bookers because they are offering only one element of the travel package.

Hotel chain web sites can lure disloyal bookers away from agency and consolidator web sites with special room rates and upgrade perks available exclusively online. Although portals have the greatest reach of all travel sites, they get the lowest percentage of bookers from all three segments. To combat online booker disloyalty, hotels, agencies and portals must take lessons from online retailers on how to encourage loyalty.

Suppliers must establish dynamic partnerships with suppliers in other travel categories that allow consumers to book flights, hotels, and car rentals at the same site. Hotel chains must sell adjacent categories of products and services. Portals should let the agencies and hotels fight over bookers and instead focus on what portals do best - offer information to consumers.

B2B applications are even bigger accelerators of change than those in the B2C space when it comes to how hospitality and travel companies will do business in the years ahead. The B2B space is populated by many types of companies, including links among supply chain partners and market exchanges selling products and services online to businesses. eProcurement is one example of a growing B2B space in the hotel industry. Adoption of B2B strategies that connect businesses in varied ways is being driven by a number of factors:

Information Technology Infrastructures

Yesterday's information technology (IT) model was based on each hotel and/or hotel group maintaining an in-house IT team, which owned and managed the business's hardware and software. Tomorrow, most businesses will have migrated to an Application Service Provision (ASP) model.

Under the ASP model, providers offer a variety of applications and services to companies, which these clients can access with nothing more than an Internet link to the ASP site. This marks a dramatic change from the traditionally defined "service bureau," which once involved the transmission of operational data to an outside agency for management by a remote application. More recently, the explosion of Internet-based software applications and services by ASP providers has caused old economy and new economy businesses alike to revisit off-premises application processing.

Wireless Application Protocol

Mature businesses are not simply assuming that a focus on eBusiness is enough. The wireless market will introduce new competitive elements. Wireless Application Protocol (WAP) is a global specification that gives wireless devices - including mobile phones, personal digital assistants (PDAs) and computer terminals—access to the Internet. The distinguishing feature of wireless service is the ability to identify a user's location.

The network seeks out the mobile phone to complete the call and knows where the holder of the phone actually is. This offers advertisers a dream channel to target customers in a personalised, time-and location-specific way. What are the potential applications or competitive threats? Looking at the customer-facing systems, there is every likelihood that WAP-enabled functionality will be developed to provide access to hotel reservation systems and loyalty traveller databases.

In the administrative areas, WAP technology can be applied to interface the mobile sales force with the centrally held customer relationship management (CRM) database—linking the revenue generating and cost generating systems in the bedroom (e.g. telephone, mini-bar, air-conditioning) to the centrally hosted property management system. .

IMPACT OF GLOBALISATION

The hospitality industry is one of the world's largest employers and arguably one of the largest traders of foreign currency. It is often also a focal point for local society, and is clearly at the center of the transfer of ideas and the cross fertilisation of cultures. At its heart, the hospitality industry plays an important part physically in bringing people together in a global community. And those countries suffering from trade imbalances due to high imports frequently look to tourism and hospitality to close the gap.

Hospitality is thus not only an industry, it is a concept—and a major force in the rapidly evolving global marketplace. The hospitality industry is thus at the very core of the globalisation of international business. Hospitality companies therefore need to consider the implications of the global context in which they operate and must be prepared to address the questions that arise from this changing environment. The globalisation of business and lifestyles is characterised by communicating over vast distances in foreign languages, frequent travel to overseas countries, dealing in many currencies, and coping with a variety of political and social systems, regulatory environments, cultures and customs.

While these aspects of globalisation are easy to identify, understanding the underlying current and future trends can be problematic. Those hospitality companies that believe that they can grow and retain a niche position without acknowledging the imperatives of globalisation need to take another look. Put another way, most hospitality businesses will need to think "globally" if they are to survive.

That goes for organisations competing in the mature European and U.S. markets, which are now seeing stiff competition from other parts of the world, especially Asia. The sheer size of the vast U.S. market, in particular, can promote an insular point of view, but hotel companies that concern themselves only with the dynamics of this domestic arena also need to hear the "wake up" call. Globalisation will ultimately touch virtually all aspects of the hospitality industry. Increasingly, customers, management processes, employees, products, and sources of capital will be competed for and will move across national boundaries. Companies which are unprepared for this will be left behind.

Local or regional entities may believe that globalisation is not their concern. But that view is in error—competition in the future will come from global entities with the advantages that globalisation brings. International hotel chains were invented after World War II; they grew in the 1960s, and expanded greatly in the following two decades. Industry and economic trends in this decade have further propelled the growth of internationally-oriented hotel companies for a variety of reasons. Severe overbuilding of hotel markets, particularly in the United States during the 1980s, halted new development almost entirely, while scarcity of growth and development opportunities in markets around the world has further supported the trend toward industry consolidation.

Many companies committed to growth have found that opportunities in their back yards have been limited because of overbuilding, and they have been forced to look beyond mature domestic markets to offshore opportunities. The pressures to expand beyond national boundaries have largely arisen from the need for growing hotel companies to reach 'critical mass'—the point at which a network of properties is sufficiently large to satisfy the travel needs of the hotel company's most valued customers.

For different companies with varying products and locations, critical mass will vary in scope. A hotel organisation, for example, may reach a point in which there is no other viable option than to expand across national boundaries if it wishes to grow, achieve critical mass and benefit from the economies of scale that accompany it. If this is the case, leadership will need to recognise the imperative of organising as a global company. As an example, consider an international hotel company that is well established in North America and Europe.

In today's world market, company leadership may cast attention on the potential for moving into burgeoning Asia/Pacific markets to compete with established regional companies. Companies considering such strategic options can succeed against strong local and regional competitors only if they capitalise on the advantages derived from being a global company. While the large international chains continue to expand on a global basis, there are in the United States a number of brand names that have yet to reach the critical mass required for marketing success.

The need for hotel companies to achieve critical mass and the attendant economies of scale suggests that we will see a diminishing number of larger companies in the future as the imperatives of global expansion persist. Economies of scale are real, not imagined, and marketing on a global basis creates a significant competitive edge. It is certain that brands and products will be increasingly marketed on a truly global basis. Growth and development functions will thus become even more critical for those organisations that have not yet achieved critical mass.

For those companies pursuing a global strategy and accustomed to hotel management contracts, franchising relationships and non-recourse financing, significant adjustments will need to be made to the growth and development model. In a number of markets around the world, the bifurcation of ownership from management and management from marketing is a concept yet to achieve real maturity.

The process that promotes these concepts is a slow one and global-minded companies will need to respond accordingly. The differences in financing, owning, operating and marketing hotel properties will thus eventually narrow in a more global environment. The challenge for companies growing into markets where local partnerships and alliances are required for success will be to convince their foreign counterparts of the benefits of structures that have been successful in their home countries.

Global Brands

The concept of projecting single brands globally is thus alluring, as well as being fully within the grasp of many hospitality companies. Nevertheless, there continues to be uncertainty about the benefits of establishing a single-brand presence in a global marketplace, in contrast to responding to the unique conditions at the local level. A number of international hotel companies have sought the economies of scale attendant to developing single brands and products, and providing them in a uniform fashion to as many markets around the globe as possible.

A countervailing trend is that many people—both tourists and business travellers—seek the unique qualities and customs of an individual locale. In response, some international hotel companies have tried to reflect local culture in the way their hotels are designed and operated. This is clearly an arena in which there is no one right answer, but rather a balance of complex factors required. For example, there is a general consensus that "global travellers," who travel frequently whether for business or recreation, usually prefer a uniform product, because they want the convenience and comfort of predictability, and they demand a high level of service.

Those who travel less frequently, but have a fairly high level of sophistication may avoid such dominant global brand and product concepts. A third group is looking for what they are accustomed to, and are attracted by brands they are familiar with; in essence, they prefer to stay in environments that reflect their home-based experience. Customer expectations are related to the level of the product, and hotel products at the lower end of the spectrum tend to be easier to standardise globally, in part because these properties are more clearly defined by physical attributes, which can be duplicated.

For the larger well-established international hotel companies that have circled the world in the quest for new opportunity, Globalisation has been a strategic concept for a number of years. International hotel companies have had to confront virtually all of the issues facing global enterprises—and in many cases more. Unlike a manufacturer with an overseas plant, for example, a hotel company must export its entire operating business to function in diverse cultural and geographic settings.

Hotel companies must have the capability of establishing an entire business concept in dramatically different local environments. As the new century approaches, formulating organisational structures that can integrate individual businesses in one seamless global structure will remain an on-going challenge. Information technology clearly is one major factor shaping the opportunities for how global hotel companies organise themselves, offering the ability to communicate with customers electronically and linking far-flung operations.

It is also clear that global organisations also benefit by becoming flatter, in contrast to pyramid-shaped structures with strong central authority. Such decentralised organisations can narrow the distance (both physical and emotional) between employers and employees, at the same time putting management and staff closer to the customer. Organisational structures that are based on hierarchical systems with authority centralised at a headquarters location, as a result, may be increasingly obsolete because they distance management from the customer, while at the same time failing to empower line management and staff responsible for delivering services.

Fortunately, "flatter" and more decentralised organisations are greatly facilitated by the increasing sophistication of technology and communications. In addition, hotel company employees represent a melting pot of cultures, customs and languages, requiring new visioning and management skills to manage effectively, as well as a commitment to education and training that is unprecedented in its breadth. Today's hotel schools will need to increase their focus on issues that have to do with a global environment—communications, international marketing and law, history, social studies, geography and language.

Company-wide training in a global organisation to assure consistent leadership, operational skills and service delivery also represents a considerable challenge. All of these factors suggest that companies expanding globally can benefit greatly by forming strategic alliances. A number of companies are moving towards such alliances with regional partners as a key strategy to provide entry to new and relatively unfamiliar markets and assure a higher level of local knowledge. Going it alone is increasingly expensive and frequently more risky.

Substantial sums of money can be spent trying to conquer a region, and there may be considerable wisdom in forging alliances with local and regional partners. Foreign hotel groups have long found it difficult to establish a U.S. presence and distribution system, for example, and will probably need to enter into alliances, rather than establishing a new product from the ground up in an extremely competitive market.

At their best, alliances capitalise on the strengths of large, multinational corporations while drawing on the benefits that tend to accrue to smaller, more differentiated companies. Creating an integrated organisation from such alliances presents a challenge, however. The overriding issue operationally is how best to maintain a firm, fixed center while encouraging flexibility and proactive approaches to local conditions. Also at issue is the choice of partner. Here, a shared operational philosophy and product/customer orientation are mandatory if the combined whole is to become bigger and more successful than the sum of the parts.

A recurrent issue for hotel companies in a global context is the need to develop global brands and image, while at the same time empowering management and staff closest to the customer in day-to-day operations. On the one hand, decentralised structures allow a hotel company to give authority to employees at the property level. Once the customer walks in the door, the service is controlled and delivered at the local level—with virtually no headquarters interface, even if those services have been centrally designed. But a key—and potentially controversial—question arises.

While operational issues must be dealt with locally, marketing is very much a corporate, chain-wide function that lends itself to realising the benefits of global structures. As a result, it is possible that the economies of scale that can be achieved by a global organisation may have less to do with operations—the running of a hotel—and much more to do with marketing. Companies need to resolve this seeming paradox. They will need to secure a balanced position between these two objectives, which are potentially conflicting—decentralisation for operational needs while taking advantage of global structures in the marketing arena.

Global Economy

Hospitality companies that wish to attract investors will need to demonstrate that they can offer better returns and performance than in the past. And, at least in the eyes of the world's financial markets, they will need to demonstrate their viability as companies in a global marketplace. For the first time real estate is now being traded as a commodity in securities markets, and we can therefore expect hospitality products in the future to be viewed in the same manner. The securitisation of real estate in the United States represents a significant trend, and it behooves savvy futurists to track these trends as they develop elsewhere in the world. Indeed, the world's financial markets are at the cutting edge of globalisation, driven by the revolution in communications.

With investment portfolios passed between the Americas, Europe and Asia/Pacific in a time continuum without interruption, 24-hour financial markets are here and are destined to impact significantly the way their customers use them. Hospitality companies that seek capital from the public marketplace (a trend which is clearly going to continue and expand) will need to function as global enterprises.

If the public markets on a global basis are going to serve corporations and produce optimum results, those public companies that feed into any or all of the three major financial centers of the world need to view themselves and to be viewed as global enterprises in order to benefit fully from what these markets have to offer. Hospitality companies that want to trade in the financial markets will need a business concept that is relatively easy to communicate and comprehend. Those companies that provide homogeneity in products and market orientations will be the most attractive to global capital markets.

Companies with simple and well-defined products such as Coca Cola have become recognised by customers and investors around the world. Hospitality companies that want to trade in the financial markets will need a business concept that is relatively easy to communicate and comprehend. A truly global enterprise will have the ability to react quickly to market opportunities, no matter where they present themselves by applying business concepts that have been proven in the context of a global undertaking. Hotel companies expanding globally will also need to confront varying traditions, structures and attitudes to property investment and valuation in different countries.

Post-Merger Integration

Post-merger integration is one area of particular importance in ensuring that the synergies promised by the deal-makers are in fact delivered after the closing. There is some evidence to suggest, however, that the benefits of merging companies can be quite elusive. One recent study of post-merger results suggested that approximately one-half of merged entities under-performed their industry rivals following the merger.

Pre-Merger

1. Drive the merger using a well-articulated overall strategy.
2. Choose a partner that fits well rather than one that happens to be available.
3. Choose a partner that is similar to you.
4. Choose a partner of a different size -same-size mergers can lead to leadership conflict.
5. Complete marketing due diligence to discover the opportunities and threats.
6. Prioritise key merger initiatives.

Post-Merger

— Provide visible leadership from top management.

— Ensure that the transition follows a structured and phased approach.

— Ensure that goals are clearly defined and progress is tracked.
— Manage change from the outset.
— Use best practices to drive the creation of the new organisation and its business processes.
— Use cross-functional teams organised to drive the merger.
— Ensure that communication is well planned and coordinated.
— Recognise that a merger is fraught with risk - avoid taking too much for granted.
— Focus on adding value to the enterprise, while avoiding those actions that can destroy it.
— Avoid the compromises that result from playing to politics.
— Concentrate on key employee retention - some folks may not have the same roles as before, but their value should be recognised and their egos nurtured.
— Identify the leadership who will make the merger work it's a very tough process and not always suitable for managers who have proven to be best at organic growth.
— Don't leave culture clashes left unchecked - culture can be pervasive and the differences in two merged companies can undermine the best laid plans for collaboration.
— The "cultural migration" to the desired organisational behavior is best achieved by visible example along with continuous reinforcement.
— IT systems are frequently incompatible—it's best to come to grips with this reality sooner rather than later.
— Recognise the importance of the company's intangible assets -customers and its own people. Mergers offer

great opportunity for competitors to raid the company for its best people and customers.

— Focus on the 80/20 rule and avoid the minutiae—over-analysing to make things perfect is generally ineffective and the delays it causes encourages resistance to change which undermines the plans when they eventually are implemented.

— And finally, don't miss the revenue enhancement opportunities through cross-selling and the development of new products and services for the expanded customer base.

For those already in post-merger mode, it will be too late to deal with the pre-merger issues outlined above. But for the here-and-now, there are clearly a number of post-merger challenges that require a great deal of attention. Those operators who take the time to deal with them proactively will probably be able to mitigate any mistakes made in the pre-merger deal-making phase.

14

Water Reduction in Hospitality Industry

Your most important resource is your employees. Not only will they have many ideas for reducing waste, but without their support it would be difficult to implement any changes successfully. Let your staff know that waste reduction is important to you, and encourage their suggestions and input. You may even choose to hold an employee contest for the best waste reduction tips!

Be sure to keep staff informed of the changes you implement, and explain why they are important. If you have started a new recycling system, are buying different, reusable products, or have switched to less toxic cleaners, for example, it's vital to train staff in their use. Make sure that your employees understand what to do—for example, there should be clear signs on the recycling bins.

Meet with your staff to ensure that everyone understands your waste reduction goals and in-house procedures. Where you can, supply incentives that will keep your staff interested and motivated in helping your business achieve its aims. Part of the money that might be saved by switching to a reusable product, for example, could go to a staff social fund, or employees who spend time helping to plan and implement new programmes could be paid overtime hours and/or be recognised with an employee service award.

PURCHASING

General Ideas

— One of the most important ways to reduce waste is to reduce excess packaging. Let your supplier know that you are serious about cutting down on unnecessary waste, and ask him or her to keep you informed of new and existing products that meet your requirements but are minimally packaged. The more restaurants that indicate a preference for less wasteful alternatives, the faster manufacturers will respond with better packaging design.

— Ask suppliers to take back and reuse their shipping boxes and pallets.

— Implementing "green" purchasing policies doesn't necessarily mean higher costs. Some environmental choices may be more expensive initially, but will often pay for themselves through reduced disposal costs. As well, some cleaners, drink mixes and other products are more economical when bought in concentrated form or in bulk, instead of ready-to-use and pre-portioned.

Beverages, Sauces, Dressings and Oils

— Serve carbonated beverages from a beverage gun or dispenser rather than from a bottle or can. If you must use bottles or cans, recycle them along with your liquor bottles.

— Buy bar mixes in concentrated form, then reconstitute them and portion them into reusable serving containers.

— Some Canadian wineries offer their cooking wine in refillable barrels. Ask your supplier to investigate this option.

— Buy and use dispenser beverages (i.e. juice, iced tea, hot chocolate) in concentrated or bulk form.

— When possible, use refillable condiment bottles and refill them from condiments purchased in bulk. This can apply to ketchup, coffee cream, sugar and other items.

Grocery, Meat, Dairy and Produce

— All foods in a restaurant must be from approved sources, so ensure that your source of organically grown foods are approved by a health inspection agency.

— Buying organically grown goods helps alleviate problems around pesticide residues, decreasing soil vitality, erosion, and farm worker health concerns. Organically produced meat, eggs, wine, coffee, fruit and vegetables are all available.

— Try to buy shelf-stable foods in bulk, but be aware of the challenges you may encounter along the way: storage problems, overflow on the floor, large or heavy containers that may be difficult for staff to handle, and chemical preservatives that may be undesirable or unnecessary. These problems aren't necessarily insurmountable, but they should be considered.

— Although buying in bulk helps reduce packaging, limited storage space in many restaurants may make this option unrealistic.

— Buy meats in the bulk or uncut form and cut to size whenever the net cost is less than if you were to buy it pre-portioned.

— Only buy meat in bulk if you have the facilities to safely cut it to size and store it.

— Consider buying eggs shelled in bulk if your egg usage for general cooking or baking is three or more cases per week. This will increase your yield (up to 30 per cent of the egg white stays with the shell when raw eggs are shelled manually) and eliminate broken eggs in the cooler, and you won't have shells or boxes to dispose of either.

— Whole shell eggs must be from inspected sources and liquid whole egg must be pasteurised.

— All eggs must be kept under refrigeration.

Paper Supplies

— Purchase paper products made from recycled materials. This could include toilet paper, paper towels, napkins, placemats, bags, menus and more. Try to find products that contain a high percentage of "post-consumer" waste: that means it's made from paper collected from residential and business recycling programmes, not just from trimmings and paper scraps from within the paper mill.

— Use straw-style stir sticks for bar beverages instead of the solid style. They usually cost less per unit and use less plastic. Additionally, use only one straw per drink, if any straw is necessary at all.

— Serve straws from health department-approved dispensers rather than offering them pre-wrapped.

— Use reusable coasters (or nothing at all) instead of paper napkins when serving beverages from the bar.

— Choose reusable coffee filters over paper ones, and unbleached paper coffee filters over bleached ones.

Janitorial and Restaurant Supplies

— Use reusable table linen, china, glass and silverware. Like china, high quality plastic place settings are also reusable, and you'll lose fewer dishes to breakage. Replace disposable stir sticks with washable spoons for coffee and tea drinkers.

— Disallow smoking or use reusable ashtrays.

— In the washrooms, use cloth roller towelling instead of paper towelling. Similarly, use cloth for kitchen and restaurant cleaning purposes, rather than paper.

— Purchase cleaning supplies in concentrate, rather than ready-to-use form. This reduces packaging waste and saves money.

— Use multi-purpose cleaners that can be used for various surfaces, rather than cleaners that are job-specific. Whenever possible, consider using cleaning agents that are either non-toxic or the least-toxic in nature.

— Use washable and reusable hats for kitchen employees instead of disposable paper ones.

— You will only be able to use re-usable china, glass and silverware if you have the proper dishwashing facilities, usually an approved commercial dishwasher.

— Although some high quality plastic dishes are re-usable, disposable plastic dishes and cutlery (intended for single use) must not be re-used.

— Hot air hand dryers in staff washrooms can also be considered in addition to cloth roller towelling to reduce re-contamination of hands.

— Although multi-purpose cleaners are generally acceptable, tasks that require sanitising of surfaces or utensils will require the use of approved sanitisers.

— When using cleaners from concentrate ensure that the diluted produce is properly labelled and stored safely away from food and food preparation areas.

Product Handling and Storage

— Check your produce deliveries carefully for rotten or damaged product, and let your supplier know if you are dissatisfied with the quality you are receiving.

— Rotate perishable stocks at every delivery to minimise waste due to spoilage. Date all products when you receive them, and put new products at the back of the shelf so older stock gets used first.

— Clean your coolers and freezers regularly to ensure that food has not fallen behind the shelving and spoiled.

— Arrange your refrigerated and dry storage areas to facilitate easy product access and rotation. This will help minimise waste due to spills, breakage and spoilage.

— Once washed, store raw vegetables and other perishables in reusable airtight containers to prevent unnecessary dehydration and spoilage. Also, store produce as far away from the condenser unit as possible to prevent freezing. Never store tomatoes and lettuce in the same container or close to each other. Tomatoes emit a gas that will turn lettuce brown.

— Order quantities carefully, but if you do end up with wilted vegetables (i.e. celery, lettuce, carrots, broccoli, etc.), reconstitute them by trimming off the very bottom part of the stalk and immersing them in warm water (about 37 degrees Celsius) for 15 to 20 minutes.

— Wrap freezer products tightly, date them, and make sure they are used in a timely fashion, to minimise waste due to freezer burn.

— Store and/or handle unwrapped paper supplies (i.e. drink cups, napkins or bags) carefully, to prevent the products from accidentally falling on the floor.

— Freeze and thaw prepared food in portion sizes that are appropriate to your needs for the day. Don't thaw a greater quantity than you'll use

— Caution must be exercised in the re-use of any leftover cream-based or other potentially hazardous foods.

Food Preparation and Storage

— Adjust inventory levels on perishables to minimise waste due to spoilage. If you are constantly throwing out a particular item that has spoiled, you are probably stocking too much of it.

— Develop hourly or daily production charts to minimise over-prepping and unnecessary waste.

— Whenever possible, prepare foods as needed in order to minimise waste due to over-preparation.

— When prepping food, only trim off what is not needed. Over-trimming typically occurs in the preparation of bulk meats and whole vegetables. Check the garbage for signs of over-trimming, and, if required, retrain your prep staff or change the products' specifications or size.

— Use vegetable and meat trimmings for soup stock.

— Pre-cool steam table hot foods in an ice bath before placing them in the cooler. Similarly, always place hot foods into clean, shallow containers before storing in the cooler. This helps prevent premature spoilage and keeps your cooler from working overtime.

— Reuse leftover cream-based sauces and soups (that have been held and stored at proper temperature) within two days of when they were originally prepared to prevent waste due to spoilage. This case also applies to leftover poultry and fishbased menu items.

— Store leftover hot foods from different stations in separate containers, rather than consolidating them, to minimise the chance of spoilage.

Equipment

— Develop and implement a monthly cleaning and maintenance programme for all your equipment. If your refrigerator, freezer, or air conditioners are being serviced, ensure that the CFCs are being treated in accordance with new provincial regulations that require recovery of ozone-depleting substances. Remember to check the air intakes on your appliances, too, where dust can cover openings. Regular maintenance of your refrigerators and freezers extends the life of the compressors, reduces energy costs and avoids food spoilages caused by breakdowns.

— Keep oven equipment calibrated to prevent over-baked products.

— Clean your fryers and filter the oil daily. This extends the life of both the fryer and the oil. Built-up carbon deposits on the bottom of the fryer act as an insulator that forces the fryer to heat longer, thus causing the oil to break down sooner.

— Use a test kit supplied by your grocery distributor in order to determine when to change your fryer oil. This is more accurate than judging by the appearance of the oil.

Production Areas

— Create staff incentives to reduce breakage or loss of china, glass and silver supplies. Employees with a "clean record" for the month could be given cash bonuses, gift certificates, a night off, or a company t-shirt, depending on your budget.

— Check for accidentally discarded china or cutlery before throwing out dining room trash.

— Place rubber mats around bus and dishwashing stations to reduce glass and china breakage—as well as injury resulting from slips.

— Have employees use non-disposable cups for their own drinks.

— Decrease your use of plastic garbage can liners by manually compacting the trash in the cans and emptying them only when they are full.

— Ensure that cracked or chipped dishware is discarded as it cannot be properly cleaned and sanitised.

Soup's On: It's a shame to throw out food that has been carefully prepared by your kitchen staff. It represents invested dollars and staff time, and a wasted resource. Avoid throwing out unused food by considering the following:

— Evaluate and adjust the size of your meal portions if they are consistently being returned unfinished.

— Offer half-portions to your guests, and a children's menu for younger diners.

— Donate any extra food to a community meal service. Food Runners will pick up your unserved portions of food and deliver them to a community kitchen or emergency shelter.

— If you can't feed people, see if you can help animals. If your restaurant is located in a rural area, there may be a nearby working or hobby farm that would be happy to use some of your leftovers, or your kitchen prep scraps. Ask your customers, or put a note on your cash register.

— If you have space, install a rodent-resistant compost bin in your back lot and compost your uncooked fruit and vegetable scraps.

The use of a service picking up scraps for processing at a centralised facility is encouraged. Approval from the local health departments must be obtained prior to installing back lot compost bins.

Dishes and Packaging

— Distribute any disposable cutlery, condiments or other accessories from behind the counter instead of offering them self-serve. Train your counter staff to dispense a predetermined quantity of these products for any meal or when requested by guests.

— Establish and advertise a policy that encourages customers to help you cut down on waste—for example, offer a 10 cent discount to people who bring their own coffee mug. As well, you can offer a 20-cup coffee card for regular customers and reward them with a reusable mug with your logo on it when the card is filled. This will encourage customer loyalty while promoting waste reduction.

— If your establishment is located in an office building or mall, consider allowing people who eat at their offices to take out their food in reusable containers. You can charge a deposit for the cutlery and china, or put a collection bin on each floor of the office building and send staff to pick up the used dishes.

— Use serving containers in sizes that meet the packaging needs of your menu items without having excess material.

— Minimise the use of unnecessary extra packaging, such as double wrapping or bagging, for dine-in or take-out foods. Establish packaging standards for every menu item and ask staff to follow them.

Recycling Activities

Recycling can reduce hotel and restaurant operating costs by diverting materials from disposal. Waste reduction can reduce purchasing costs in addition to disposal costs. Recycling demonstrates a hotel or restaurant's commitment to environmental protection to customers, businesses and employees. Recycling saves raw materials, energy and reduces environmental pollution.

— Recycling glass saves 25-32% of the energy used to make virgin glass.

— Recycling paper uses 60% less energy than manufacturing paper from virgin timber and reduces pollutants by 50%.

— Recycling steel and tin cans saves 74% of the energy used to produce them from raw materials.

— Recycling steel reduces energy consumption by 70%.

— Recycling aluminium uses 95% less energy than producing aluminium products from raw materials.

To reduce waste:

— Set up a rendering service for your waste grease, fat or used cooking oil.

— Set up a cardboard and/or glass recycling programme with a local recycler.

— Make sure staff are flattening tin and aluminium cans before putting them in the recycling bin. By reducing the volume of recyclables, you will save money by decreasing the frequency of pick-ups by your recycling contractor.

— Donate empty plastic pails or buckets to schools, nurseries or churches, or offer them to your customers.

— Donate old uniforms to theatre companies and thrift shops.

Your environmental efforts are not only likely to attract customers, they will encourage other restaurants to follow your example. Publicise your efforts in some of the following ways:

— Keep a tally of your waste reduction progress and post a chart so customers can see how well you're doing.

— List your environmental efforts on your menu, and if your menu is printed on recycled paper, be sure it says so.

— Encourage customer awareness by offering a donation to an environment group when people purchase the special of the day or bring their own reusable mug. You might also act as a distribution point for free environmental brochures or publications.

— Once your programme is successfully underway, contact your local media.

Environmental Policy Development

To assure that your programme will be successful, develop an environmental statement incorporating recycling into your company policies.

Support from the top of an organisation is key to the success of your recycling programme. Managers need to understand why it's important to have a recycling programme; they also need to know how a programme will positively impact the business operations overall. Management endorsement of an environmental policy ensures that resources will be available when needed. A policy also sends a message to all employees that the company is serious about the recycling programme. This commitment will help to promote a similar attitude among the establishment's employees and customers. An effective programme will need the full support of every employee as well as a determination to make it work.

First steps:

— Write a company policy statement that reflects the commitment of top management.

— Set reduction goals that are specific and measurable, such as a 25% reduction in garbage hauled away within the next 6 months.

— Communicate this policy so that it is clear to all staff.

Implementing the policy

For smaller businesses: Appoint a recycling coordinator to manage the entire recycling programme. The person selected should be genuinely interested in recycling and able to interface with personnel at all organisation levels. It is advisable to incorporate recycling responsibilities into the employee's job description.

For larger businesses: Establish a "Green Team" that will develop and implement the programme. Choose representatives from the departments that will be most affected by your recycling programme. It is also a good idea to have a spokesperson for the employees. The team should have frequent meetings to discuss how their department is doing and ways of improving the programme.

Waste Audit

An audit is a simple assessment of the type and quantities of waste that the business generates. It can help you decide which materials can be recycled and how many collection containers will be necessary. Not all hotels or restaurants are the same. The amount of waste and recyclables produced is affected by variables that differ from one business to the next. You need to examine your own waste stream before adopting new programmes to assure a good fit with your business.

One approach is to sort and weigh several samples of your trash over time. This effort will provide a good accounting of your waste stream composition. Another method involves a review of purchasing and waste removal records. These records can help you to develop a decent estimate of your waste materials. Look for high-volume materials such as corrugated cardboard, and for high-value materials such as toner cartridges and aluminium cans. These types of materials make good candidates for waste reduction and recycling. Walk through the facility noting what type of waste is discarded in each area. A walk-through will help you determine the size and placement of collection bins.

Typical Wastes

The type and mix of wastes that your facility generates will be unique. Below shows some typical materials found in restaurants and hotels.

— *Office Area*: office paper, corrugated paper or cardboard, other paper, beverage cans and bottles

— *Dining Area*: beverage cans and bottles, newspaper, uneaten food

— *Kitchen*: food waste, grease/oil, packaging waste like corrugated cardboard, pallets, steel cans, aluminium cans, glass and plastic bottles

— *Guest Rooms*: newspaper, magazines, bottles, cans

A key reason for starting a recycling programme is to reduce waste collection costs. After implementing your recycling programme, you need to conduct a second waste audit to see if your programme has significantly reduced the amount of waste generated. If it has, you may want to reduce your collection schedule or the size of your container to save money on refuse disposal costs.

Reduce and Reuse

Prevent waste creation by reusing items and reducing your consumption of resources. Save money on disposal by not creating waste in the first place. The hierarchy of solid waste management calls for reduction and reuse before recycling. Now that you have finished the initial waste audit, you can identify materials for reuse and reduction. Below are some techniques for restaurants and hotels.

Purchasing

— Ask suppliers to take packaging back.

— Ask your suppliers to inform you of products that contain recycled content, have reduced packaging, and are packaged in recyclable materials.

— Establish purchasing guidelines to encourage the use of durable, repairable equipment, and reusable products such as linen and tableware.

— Buy a dispensing system to replace disposable room amenities such as shampoo and lotion bottles.

Donation

— Guest hangers no longer suitable for use to local dry cleaners.

— Linens, towels, blankets, soap, shampoo, uniforms, and used furniture to a local shelter.

— Egg cartons, strawberry baskets, tennis ball canisters, poster board, and other materials to schools or daycare centers for use in arts and crafts activities.

— Flowers that were used for a banquet to a local hospice or hospital.

— Unserved food to local food banks. Produce scraps can be composted on site or donated to local farmers for composting.

Waste minimisation

— Use pourers for sugar, pitchers for cream and small serving dishes for butter and jellies.

— Use cloth towels or hot air dryers in the restrooms.

— Buy beverages in concentrate or bulk form.

— Use health department-approved, refillable condiment dispensers instead of individual packets

— Minimise excessive use of disposable and non-recyclable packaging.

— Use minimal packaging to wrap take-out items and offer pre-packaged food in recyclable packaging.

— Buy shelf-stable food supplies in bulk.

— Have employees use permanent-ware mugs or cups for their drinks.

— Use straw-style stir sticks for bar beverages instead of the solid style.

— Serve straws from health department approved dispenser rather than pre-wrapped, and offer only one straw per drink.

— Offer customers a discount if they bring their own mugs, containers, or bags.

— Print daily specials on a chalkboard or dry-erase board, rather than printing daily specials on new sheets of paper every day.

Reuse

— Store food in reusable containers

— Use old paper bags when draining fat off oily foods, instead of paper towels.

— Turn stained tablecloths into napkins and chef's aprons. Use cloth linens and old linens for rags.

— Use reusable coffee filters. Quality cotton, silk or metal filters can replace the cartons of paper filters restaurants go through in a given year.

— Collect and resell used cooking fat (oils) back to a manufacturer.

Food preparation and storage

— Adjust inventory levels on perishables to reduce waste due to spoilage or dehydration.

— Use daily production charts to minimise over prepping and unnecessary waste.

— Whenever possible, prepare foods to order.

— Adjust the size of meal portions if you find they are consistently being returned unfinished.

— Wrap freezer products tightly, label, and date them. Make sure they are used in a timely fashion, to minimise waste due to freezer burn.

— Check your produce deliveries carefully for rotten or damaged product, and return any substandard product.

— Rotate perishable stock at every delivery to minimise waste due to spoilage.

— Clean coolers and freezers regularly to ensure that food has not fallen behind the shelving and spoiled.

— Arrange your refrigerated and dry storage areas to facilitate easy product access and rotation.

What and Where to Recycle

Identify eligible materials for recycling

Selecting Recyclables: Based on your waste audit findings, you can now select potential materials for recycling. If an item was not a candidate for waste reduction or reuse, you may be able to keep it out of your trash dumpster with a recycling programme. You will have to work with a hauler offering recycling services to determine which materials will be economical to recycle. The following materials are common recyclables collected by hotels and restaurants.

— *Paper*:
  - — computer paper
  - — bond paper
  - — corrugated cardboard boxes
  - — newspaper
  - — telephone books
  - — magazines

— *Metal*:
  - — aluminium cans
  - — tin/steel cans

— *Glass*:
  - — clear, brown, green bottles and jars

— *Plastics*:
  - — narrow neck bottles

— *Office*:
  - — copier and printer cartridges

— *Maintenance*:
  - — motor oil
  - — antifreeze
  - — paint

— *Other*:
  - — wood pallets
  - — polystyrene containers

Collection tips

A good collection system will help you capture a high percentage of your recyclables. Read the following tips for ideas.

— Be sure that recycling and trash bins look different from each other and are clearly marked. Both types of bins should be conveniently located in the kitchen and bar areas so that employees will use them.

— If your establishment is self-serve, post signs letting customers know that you are recycling and what they should do with their bottles and cans. Either put out a bin for these items, or have customers leave them on a designated counter for collection by your staff.

— If space is a problem, specially designed equipment such as can, glass and plastic crushers are available to reduce the volume of your recyclable materials.

— Some fast food chains are operating recycling programmes for polystyrene containers.

— Make sure that bins in public areas are well-marked. It is best to choose bins with specialised openings, such as a hole for cans or a slot for newspapers, for these areas.

— Hotels and motels should recycle the "wet" and "dry" materials received through their offices, guest rooms, restaurants, and cafeterias. Dry recyclables, from offices and guest rooms, include different grades of paper. Wet recyclables, from the restaurants and cafeterias, include cans and bottles as well as food waste, which can be used for pig chow or for composting in some areas of the country.

— Set up appropriate recycling programmes in administrative offices, food service areas, guest rooms and public areas. It is best to concentrate on areas that produce significant amounts of particular materials.

— Set up a log book or a receipt system to record the volume of recyclables leaving the premises. This will enable you to receive proper compensation for your materials and to take appropriate action if volumes decrease.

— The wood pallet and container industry is the largest user of hardwood lumber. Recycled pallets are used for poultry litter, livestock bedding, fuel, mulch, soil amendment, particle board, and furniture.

Contamination

Contamination turns your carefully separated recyclables back into garbage. Keep your recyclables clean. Locating the recycling containers near trash cans can cut down on contamination. Clearly mark all collection containers and make it as difficult as possible to contaminate the recyclables. For example, use lids with only a small hole in the top for the collection of aluminium cans.

Talk to Your Hauler

Recycling issues

It is important to explore what types of recycling opportunities the contractor can provide. Depending on market conditions, the disposal contractor may pay you for your recycled product, haul it away at no extra charge, or provide reduced rates for containers and periodic pick-ups. If your business generates a lot of recyclables, it is important to explore this issue carefully since some firms may offer much better prices for recyclables.

Your waste hauler can help you set up your recycling programme by suggesting appropriate containers to use and by providing educational materials for your employees. Ask your waste hauler for advice about keeping recyclables and wet waste separate. Depending on the company's trucks and equipment, your hauler may want to give you separate containers for trash and recyclables. It's important to properly sort and prepare your recyclables. If you don't, recyclables become garbage. If your business generates a small amount of recyclables, you may find that private haulers will not be interested in collecting your materials.

In this situation it is often beneficial to join together with neighbouring businesses to consolidate your recyclables and get better prices. Another option for small businesses is to check with local governments to see if they will accept commercial recyclables at their public recycling drop-off centers. These centers are typically intended for residential use.

Disposal issues

Even with a good recycling programme, your business will still generate trash for disposal. Since recycling will reduce the amount of trash, you should be able to save on disposal expenses. Ask prospective haulers to estimate these savings and to help you to choose the appropriate refuse container. Containers are usually offered in sizes of two, four, six, eight and 10 cubic yards. Generally, you can expect to pack seven or eight filled trash bags per cubic yard.

Depending on how quickly the container gets filled, the disposal contractor should be able to time pick-ups accordingly. While scheduled weekly pick-up is quite common, larger businesses may want service several times a week. In contrast, smaller businesses may simply want to schedule pick-up on an on-call basis. If your company falls in this small category, you should learn how quickly the contractor will respond to a call for pickup.

Pricing for disposal and recycling services

Pricing for disposal and recycling services will help your decide which materials to recycle. Most disposal contractors offer monthly pricing, which incorporates a rental fee for the container, a set charge per pickup, additional charges or credits for recycling, and optional services like weekend pick-up or rush service. Contractors typically encourage customers to enter at least a three-year agreement, but many will consider working with you for a term as short as one year. Competition for disposal and recycling services can be quite fierce, so shopping around for the best deal usually pays off.

Tips for saving money:

— *Receive multiple bids*—the disposal industry is highly competitive.

— *Share the costs*—if there are other businesses nearby, you may want to consider sharing a container.

— *Be sure that your container can be easily secured against unauthorised usage*—you do not want to pay for someone else's trash.

— *Break down your trash*—the disposal charge is based on the container size rather than the amount of waste generated. You can often save money by using a smaller container and packing the container more efficiently.

Buying recycled

Buying recycled products creates demand for the recyclables that your business collects. Collection of recyclables is only part of the economic process that makes recycling successful. The other key activities are reprocessing the materials into new products and selling these products in the marketplace. If no one buys recycled-content products, there will be no demand for the cans, bottles and paper that your business generates and the prices paid for these materials will fall accordingly. This relationship explains why it is important for your business to buy recycled-content products.

Table 1. Recycled-Content Products

Paper Products	
paper towels	facial tissue
toilet tissue	toilet seat covers
office paper	menu paper
napkins	place mats
cardboard	
Glass Products	
bottles and jars	floor tiles
Metal Products	
steel cans	aluminium cans
Plastic Products	
carpets	desk sorters
desk trays	pencil holders
binders	plastic envelopes
trash can linersflower pots	
bottles and containers	scouring pads
auto parts	paint brushes
industrial paints	trash cans
recycling bins	kitchen drain boards
drums and pails	matting
milk bottle carriers	industrial pallets
bathroom stalls	plastic lumber
Others	
toner cartridges and printer ribbons	

Interesting new products are being manufactured from your recyclables and turning up in the marketplace. Products range from ordinary writing paper to decorative glass tiles. The list on the following page provides some examples. Look for products with high "post-consumer content." Post-consumer means that the item's recycled content comes from products that have been previously used and sent for recycling. Pre-consumer content refers to material that has never been sold to consumers, but collected from factory processes and reused to make products. For most printing and writing paper, look for at least 20% post-consumer content.

Talk with whoever purchases your supplies and also sit down with your vendors. Recycled-content products can have equal or superior quality to virgin material products. As with any purchase, it is important to assess the quality of each product on an individual basis. Sometimes, purchasing policies are so strict that they needlessly exclude the consideration of some recycled products. Review your existing purchasing policies to assure they do not prevent the purchase of these goods. Specify the use of recycled content products in all printing and janitorial contracts. State that your organisation expects vendors to supply products with recycled content.

Determine the collection strategy

You can determine the location of recycling collection containers and who will be responsible for transporting and emptying them. A guiding principle is to make it as convenient as possible. The system must be both simple and reliable to ensure long-term success. Glass, metal, plastic and food wastes should be separated in the kitchen and bar areas. Different coloured containers can be effective to help the staff separate the materials by type. Keeping garbage and recycling containers separated avoids confusion and is a good way to improve the efficiency of your recycling efforts.

Separating also helps the chef and management to be aware of what is in the trash (i.e. good food wasted, silverware in trash, amount of glass breakage, etc.). Office paper recycling, including front desk, hostess station and cashier, increases significantly when collection begins at each desk. Employees sort recyclable paper into special containers beside or on their desks and then empty them into central collection containers located throughout the building. Multiple containers may be provided to sort multiple grades of paper.

Central collection containers should be placed in convenient locations, close to areas where materials are generated, Key locations include: all kitchen areas, bars, offices, copy room and store room. At least one central container for every working area is recommended. The size of container must be appropriate for the number of guests and employees served, amount of recyclables generated and collection frequency. Recycling containers should be clearly labelled to avoid any confusion. Trash cans should also be available at those sites in order to minimise unwanted trash (contamination) in recycling containers.

A designated storage area is required to store the materials to be recycled. This area should be easily accessible to both your recycling service and to those responsible for transferring recyclables from the central collection bins. Do not overlook available outdoor locations. Containers should have tight fitting lids or covers and may need to be in an enclosed area if outdoors. Recycling dealers require that corrugated cardboard cartons be broken down or baled.

Balers may be provided by the recycler, purchased or rented, depending upon circumstances. Balers are available in various sizes and may be placed either indoors or outside in a covered area. Use of a baler significantly reduces the amount of space required to store cardboard and paper waste and saves time by eliminating the need for employees to break down cardboard boxes.

Obtain Containers: Storage containers may be provided by your hauler or available for lease as part of their service. Containers are also available through a variety of other sources. Information can be obtained from the Full Circle Resources consultants. A wide variety of recycling container styles are available. Any container, such as a 55 gallon drum, may be affixed with the recycling logo for use as a recycling container. Your hauler will inform you of any special requirements.

Education and Promotion

Educate your employees and customers about your recycling programme. Education of your employees and customers should help guarantee the success of your recycling programme. For the programme to excel, workers need to consistently follow the rules about separating material. Sometimes customers may also get involved. At minium, businesses should promote their recycling programme to their customers as a sign of efficiency and environmental stewardship. Over time, people may forget the policies—repetition, reminders and promotion is an ongoing process. Some education tips appear below.

Employees

— Provide education as part of new employee orientation.

— Tell your staff what you hope to accomplish recycling.

— Periodically reinforce education during staff meetings.

— Have special training for janitorial staff on how to consolidate material for the hauler.

— Empower janitorial staff to monitor the programme for any new problems.

— Train grounds crews to handle yard waste.

— Make a DO and DON'T list for recyclables and post it near work stations.

— Remember to ask your staff for their input—include them in the decision process to encourage participation.

Customers

— Promote your programme in-house with charts and posters.

— Include information in your advertising.

— Mention the programme in your guest information packets.

— Always put a recycling container next to a garbage can .

— Make recycling bins stand out.

Waste Sort Instruction

Begin the waste sort:

— Assemble your waste sample in a location that is convenient, large enough for this activity, and available for the duration of the sample. Your sample may be one day's worth of waste or a representative sample from each department. A multi-day sampling is suggested if there is a large potential for daily variations.

— Weigh the empty containers in which the sorted materials will be placed and note the weight on both the container and waste sort form.

— Sort the waste by the components your restaurant has chosen to quantify.

— Your restaurant may want to separate the major components into subcategories (i.e. sorting glass into the subcategories of clear, green and brown).

— Place the sorted materials into the empty containers.

Complete the waste sort:

— Weigh each of the filled containers (partial and/or full) and note in "Full Container Weight" column on form.

— Record the empty weight of containers in "Empty Container Weight" column on form.

— Subtract "Empty Container Weight" from "Full Container Weight" to get "Net Waste Component Weight". Record weight in "Net Waste Component Weight" column.

— Add all the net component weights to get the "Total Waste Weight". Record this total figure in the respective "Totals" column and also in the "Total Waste Generated" column.

— Divide Net Component Weight by the Total Waste Generated and multiply by 100 to compute the Component Percentage.

15

Trends and Opportunities in Hospitality Industry

Following a growth of 8.5% in 2003/04, the Indian economy performed extremely well during 2004/05, with GDP growing at 6.9%. Despite the anticipated growth in GDP in real terms for 2004/ 05 being less than that for 2003/04, it is among the highest achieved since Independence. In the first quarter of the current fiscal (2005/06), the economy registered an impressive growth of 8.1%.

Domestic political stability and a benign world economic environment have provided a backdrop conducive to development, while a strong growth momentum in the Industry (especially manufacturing) and Services sectors has provided the impetus necessary to sustain a strong performance in the short to medium term. Another positive feature has been the continued maintenance of relative stability of prices and control on inflation despite a rising world fuel price regime.

While the Reserve Bank of India has projected a GDP growth of 7.0% for 2005/06, following the economy's first quarter performance, projections made by independent agencies anticipate a GDP increase of 7.5-8.0%. While agriculture and allied activities are the main source of livelihood for 58% of India's population, the share of this sector in the overall economy has declined steadily over the past few decades, from 36.6% of GDP in 1983/84 to 22.8% in 2003/04.

The Index of Industrial Production, which measures the overall industrial growth rate, was 10.1% in October 2004, compared to 6.2% in October 2003. The share of Industry in the overall economy has remained stable over the past few decades from 25.8% of GDP in 1983/84 to 26.4% in 2003/04. The Services sector has maintained a steady growth pattern since 1996/97, except for a decline in 2000/01. The share of Services in the overall economy has increased greatly over the past few decades, from 37.6% of GDP in 1983/84 to 50.7% in 2003/04.

Trade, hotels, transport & communications witnessed their highest-ever growth of 10.9% in 2004, followed by financial services. Together, they constitute about one-half of the Services sector. This sector is presently the largest contributor of room nights for hotels in India, and its continued growth has greatly influenced the current boom in demand, particularly in the National Capital Region (comprising Delhi, Gurgaon, NOIDA and some other surrounding areas), as well as in Bangalore, Hyderabad, Pune, Chennai and Mumbai.

India's GDP growth over the next few years would continue to be driven by Services and international trade. Within Services, the key sectors that would spearhead growth are aviation, retail and commercial real estate, ITeS, telecom, insurance, and financial services. This growth in Services is expected to further increase demand for hotel rooms of all categories across the country.

Economists reported that India now ranks second, after China, as a location for foreign investment in manufacturing. This is a rise from the sixth place at which it was ranked a year ago. India's foreign exchange reserves, stand at an estimated level of nearly US$143 billion, as of September 2005. Inflation, which was at a four-year high of 8.0% in early September 2004, was 3.75% in September 2005. High international oil prices, the highest ever with crude oil trading at US$70 a barrel and fluctuating between US$60 and US$70, are expected to lead to significant widening of the merchandise trade deficit. The Rupee is expected to remain stable against the US Dollar in 2005/06 with the widening of the US fiscal trade deficit.

Tourism: Trends and Developments

The year 2004 has been the best year till date for inbound travel, with foreign visitor arrivals reaching a record 3.40 million, resulting in international tourism receipts of US$4.8 billion. This impressive performance in tourist arrivals is attributable to a strong sense of business and investment confidence in India: inspired by steady growth in the Indian economy, a strong performance of the domestic corporate sector, as well as initiatives taken to make peace with Pakistan, strengthen ties with other nations and open sectors of the economy to private sector/foreign investment.

Significantly, the bulk of international arrivals in India, both in 2003 and 2004, have been business travellers. The continued focus on liberalising the Indian aviation sector has provided a further impetus to travel. Domestic air passenger traffic grew by 24.2% in 2004/05 compared to 2003/04. International passenger traffic observed a growth of 16.7% in the same period. The increase in international flights, seat capacity and frequency into the country and the decision to allow private airlines like Jet Airways and Air Sahara to fly abroad will also have a positive impact on tourist and business arrivals in India, as it will provide additional seats to key destinations.

Increase in charter flights into India and new airlines providing additional seats for travel within the country are expected to have a significant impact on increasing affordable air travel within the country. Furthermore, India's growing recognition as an exciting place to visit has helped boost its image as a leisure destination. While the encouraging trend in foreign tourist arrivals has attracted much attention, very little has actually been said about domestic tourism. Domestic tourism, according to our estimates, grew by 40% on an annual basis over the last three years and is currently estimated at 230 million travellers. A rise in disposable income across most income segments, and a corresponding increase in the propensity to spend, together with more affordable air travel, have fuelled this growth.

Rising affluence and higher incomes are also expected to enhance the concept of travelling for leisure. Domestic travel, both business and leisure, also benefited from a strong performance of the corporate sector in India, and the overall sense of optimism with regard to the economy. The current government, like its predecessor, is adopting a proactive strategy towards the development of tourism in India. The continued Incredible India campaign has had a strongly positive impact on tourist arrivals. Definite efforts are being made to communicate the Brand India message: as the host, India made its presence strongly felt at the World Travel & Tourism Council (WTTC)-promoted Global Travel & Tourism Summit held in New Delhi in early April this year (2005).

There is also an increasing focus on promoting traditional tourist destinations in the country and on prioritising new attractions and travel circuits. Niche marketing in areas such as medical and health tourism, is expected to be a major growth driver. These segments generated 150,000 visitors in 2003, a number that is expected to increase to 1 million, and bring in revenues up to US$5 billion in a few years. Prospects for tourism in India, both inbound and domestic, are bright, with many opportunities.

According to recent estimates of the World Travel & Tourism Council (as of early 2005), Indian tourism demand will grow at 8.8% over the next ten years, which would place India as the second most rapidly growing tourism market in the world after Montenegro and before China. This is expected to result in a growth of 7.1% in total travel and tourism GDP and an increase of 0.9% in travel and tourism employment.

The HVS International survey has been computed by dividing the respondent branded hotels into their respective classifications according to star grading. The demand for quality accommodation from all market segments, especially the commercial and extended-stay markets, continued to be higher than the additions to supply resulting in acute demand-supply imbalance in certain cities, such as Bangalore, Mumbai and Delhi (NCR). This demand-supply imbalance enabled hotels in these cities to charge higher tariffs across all market segments. As a result, the industry saw a 12-month growth of 20.7% in average rate (in 2004/05), compared to a 12-month occupancy growth of 7.1%.

Over the past five years, additions to room supply have mostly been contributed by developments in the budget and mid-market segments. The increased representation of branded hotels in these segments during weak demand periods resulted in a downward spiralling of average rates, thus lowering overall average rate figures for the industry. The year 2004/05 was marked by an improvement in average rate—spurred by strong rate growth trends in the budget and mid-market segments. The highest annual growth in average rate, in Rupee terms, was witnessed in the four-star (25.7%) and five-star (24.2%)

categories followed by the five-star deluxe category (19.2%).

The average rate for three-star properties showed a lower increase (12.5%). It may also be noted that, over a ten-year period, the compounded average rate growth in Rupee terms has been strongest in the four-star category followed by five-star and three-star hotels. Hotels across all categories have witnessed an improved foreign domestic guest ratio and, therefore, despite a stronger Rupee, the growth in average rate in US Dollar terms has been higher across all categories. Average occupancy witnessed an across-the-board growth, for the third consecutive year. Strong year-round demand from the commercial travel segment compounded by higher demand from segments.

The emergence of relatively new feeder markets and consistent demand from niche markets, such as the extended-stay segment, have resulted in a higher level of base demand that ensures a minimum level of occupancy. This demand has been extremely advantageous, as it enabled hotels to indulge in proactive yield management, rate contracting and micro segment planning. Five-star deluxe hotels witnessed the largest increase in occupancy (8.8%), followed by five-star hotels (7.3%). Growth for the four-star and three-star categories was 5.7% and 2.7%, respectively.

Occupancy levels have shown a smaller increase this year (compared to 2003/04), as markets now have a higher base against which to benchmark their growth. In terms of RevPAR (Rooms Revenue per Available Room), all star categories experienced healthy growth in 2004/05. Fivestar hotels experienced the maximum growth in Rupee terms (33.3%) followed by four-star hotels (32.9%) and five-star deluxe hotels (29.7%). The three-star segment witnessed the least improvement (15.5%). In US Dollar terms the five-star segment showed the highest increase (36.6%), followed by the four-star (36.1%) and five-star deluxe (32.9%) segments.

In 2004/05, Ahmedabad saw the highest occupancy growth (16.8%), followed by Agra (16.4%) and Jaipur (14.3%). For the second year in a row Agra and Jaipur, both part of the much-popular Golden Triangle, witnessed their highest occupancy increase, thanks to sustained demand from domestic travellers and higher foreign tourist arrivals. Demand for the Goa market continues to remain strong when we take into account the supply addition during 2002/03.

Occupancy growth in Goa was 5.9% in 2004/05. The NCR currently has among the largest number of branded hotel rooms in the country and occupancy grew by an impressive 8.1%, indicating strong demand trends across all market segments and feeder markets. Mumbai, on the other hand, witnessed a 3.9% increase. During 2004/05, marketwide occupancy for Mumbai showed a much flatter growth; this can be attributed to a larger room inventory, owing to an increase in supply, especially in the branded five-star deluxe and five-star categories. Contrary to market perceptions, the cyber cities of Bangalore and Hyderabad had the lowest annual growth in occupancy amongst the ten cities.

Bangalore witnessed a small increase of 2.5% while the Hyderabad market grew only at 2.2%. The lack of room availability continues to be acute in these markets resulting in a huge level of unaccommodated demand, which is now being catered to by standalone hotels and serviced apartments. Also, the existing rates in markets such as Bangalore are compelling a large section of corporate travellers to make adjustments in terms of their hotel preferences. In terms of average rate (Rupee terms), Bangalore continues to be the rate leader for the second consecutive year, witnessing a rate growth of 63.1% in 2004/05. Riding on strong corporate and extended-stay demand, Hyderabad witnessed a rate increase of 25.7%.

Moreover, for the first time in ten years, highly seasonal markets such as Ahmedabad, Agra, Jaipur and Goa all witnessed an annual growth of 20.0% or higher. This is an astonishing achievement and points to the strong potential offered by secondary markets and leisure destinations for new hotel development, in the present scenario of robust demand trends and very low room inventory. The four main metro cities—Delhi, Mumbai, Chennai and Kolkata—continued to witness a steady improvement in average rate for the second year in a row. Average rate growth in Delhi was 21.8% while rates in Mumbai went up by 13.8%. Chennai and Kolkata, which have traditionally remained price sensitive markets, witnessed a modest growth of 10.2% and 6.4%, respectively. In US Dollar terms, growth in average rate in 2004/05 was highest for Bangalore (67.6%), followed by Hyderabad (30.0%).

Agra, Ahmedabad, Goa and Jaipur witnessed growth in the 20.0% range. The Kolkata and Chennai markets registered the lowest increase. Based on the development status of various hotel projects across the ten cities studied, our assessment is that over the next 24-36 months, most hotels across star categories will be able to maximise yields and prices will move up. Our research indicates that the majority of hotel markets in India follow a one-year lag period before rates start moving upwards; for the next three years, most markets have the potential to register average annual growth in the range of 20-25%. The planned addition to supply will start a rate rationalisation process and rates are likely to flatten starting the last quarter of 2007.

In terms of RevPAR growth in 2004/05, Bangalore (67.3%) was in number one position, followed by Agra

(44.4%), Ahmedabad (42.8%) and Jaipur (38.2%). The emergence of secondary markets as RevPAR leaders has taken place for the first time, pointing to the potential of these locations for hotel development. The four metro cities also performed well in terms of RevPAR, with the NCR market appreciating by 31.6%, Mumbai growing by 18.2%, and Chennai and Kolkata showing an increase of 18.6% and 17.7%, respectively. In the short term, RevPAR performance in primary markets

that include the four metros, Bangalore and Hyderabad is likely to be a function of rate improvements in each individual markets. These cities have realised their peak potential in terms of occupancy growth, and further increases are likely to follow a much flatter growth trajectory. Due to the limited availability of rooms, these markets will witness higher average rate growth.

RevPAR performance in secondary destinations, both commercial and leisure, will depend upon demand growth from key markets and occupancy improvement is likely to be the most important driver. Secondary markets, typically, have substantially higher rate sensitivity, resulting in longer rate maturity periods.

Hotel Supply

In the past year, much has been talked about the insufficient inventory of quality accommodation across India. The recent boom witnessed many hotel markets in India and expectations of strong room night demand in the forthcoming years has brought about a renewed interest on the part of real estate developers in hotel projects. In the last one year, several new hotels have been announced in high-growth markets such as Bangalore, Hyderabad and Gurgaon.

Market surveys conducted recently by HVS at the above three locations have identified 65 hotel projects, under various stages of development, that will together provide an additional inventory of approximately 13,500 rooms. Taking into account the nature of demand, customer demographics, key feeder markets and market segmentation we believe that Bangalore, Hyderabad and Gurgaon would be close to saturation, should all the planned supply actually be developed. The cumulative addition to supply for Mumbai, Chennai and Kolkata is likely to be 35 hotels with an inventory of 8,000 rooms.

The demand for hotel accommodation in the latter three markets has been determined using a mixed portfolio of market segments and diverse key feeder markets. The lack of seasonality also improves these cities' overall potential and our estimate is that the planned supply will be readily absorbed, taking into account projections of double-digit annual demand growth over a three to five year horizon. In Mumbai, for example, while new hotels have commenced operations in the last three to four years, strong demand conditions have ensured consistent marketwide growth, both in terms of average rate and occupancy.

An encouraging development in 2004/05 has been the number of hotel projects announced in secondary cities such as Pune, Jaipur, Agra and Ahmedabad. Unlike metro cities, which are expected to witness new room additions to an existing mature level of room inventory, the secondary markets will grow from a much smaller base. Thus, supply additions are not likely to impact market occupancies, owing to large levels of unaccommodated demand that would be absorbed by the planned supply. A classic example is that of Goa, where the total room inventory in the branded hotel segment literally doubled, between 2002 and 2003.

Industry observers had indicated that marketwide performance would suffer tremendously. Instead, the addition to supply was matched with strong year round demand from domestic inbound travel and MICE segments, the market continued to perform well and is now on a consistent growth curve. Going forward, the biggest challenge, given the present supply scenario, will be the availability of quality sites for hotel projects.

Site location, accessibility, visibility and proximity to key demand areas are critical factors for long terms feasibility of hotels and lack of good sites would have a negative impact on the supply front. The real estate market, too, has seen its best times in the last two years, and existing land prices across most cities are somewhat prohibitive, especially for standalone property developers.

Future Trends in Indian Hospitality Industry

Having researched various markets and conducted surveys for the past nine years, we have had a unique opportunity to understand hotel industry trends that have now witnessed a complete cycle. The industry was at its peak during 1995/96 and maintained a consistent trend over the following three years. In 1999, India carried out a nuclear weapons test; this was soon followed by the Kargil conflict between India and Pakistan.

Relations between the two countries were unfriendly and this uncertainty had a huge impact on travel. From 2001 onwards, a series of international events such as 9/11, the SARS outbreak and the US war in Iraq further affected commercial demand and international tourist traffic. Hotel markets across most of the world witnessed an occupancy decline; however, in India, this impact was for a relatively smaller time period. Strong demand from domestic leisure travel and continued travel within India, especially business travel, enabled hotel demand to grow. In 2003/ 04, most hotel markets had recovered, across all star categories, and were recording impressive growth in terms of occupancy.

In the last 12-18 months, hotel operators have been able to optimise demand and implement proactive rate management strategies. The average rate performance in the majority of markets clearly reflects this. With projections of strong demand growth and limited addition to supply expected, most cities are likely to maintain high occupancies and witness average rate growth in the range of 25-30%, annually, for the next three years.

Comparisons with the corresponding period last year have also been presented, to illustrate the extent of change. Performance trends for the first five months of 2005 are encouraging. Most markets that have registered strong growth are continuing to show marginal increase in occupancy accompanied by very strong rate performance. In 2004/05, occupancy growth in Kolkata and Chennai was much flatter; these markets showed impressive gains more recently, in the first quarter of 2005.

Rate growth in these markets does not mirror demand growth; as mentioned earlier, Kolkata and Chennai have traditionally been rate sensitive markets and we estimate that both cities will see strong rate growth from the third quarter of 2005. Occupancy growth for Hyderabad has been small and Bangalore actually had a small decline in occupancy despite a decrease in room supply due to renovations.

However, it is the same demand-supply imbalance that continues to allow hotels in Bangalore to charge rates in the US$250 to US$300 range and our estimate is that in the next financial year, rates in both markets (Bangalore and Hyderabad) will grow at approximately 20-25%. With new supply being phased in starting early 2007, there will be rate consolidation, and both rate and occupancy are expected to stabilise by 2008.

Interestingly, Goa remains the most underestimated market among the major cities and we have been recommending this market for development for the past 2-3 years. It continues to see the highest demand growth in the current year with reasonably strong average rate increase. In terms of RevPAR the market, in the first five months of 2005, has grown by 55.2%, second only to New Delhi (64.3%) and slightly ahead of Hyderabad (52.6%).

Mumbai and Delhi continue to witness strong commercial demand and we expect annual occupancy growth in the region of 12-15% accompanied by 20-25% growth in average rates in 2005/ 06. The Commonwealth Games to be hosted in New Delhi in 2010 is also likely to induce strong demand and greatly assist in the absorption of additional supply in the market. A buoyant economy, robust corporate results and a booming stock market are strong indicators for surging domestic leisure demand. Foreign tourist arrivals have grown by 16.0% for first eight months of 2005.

The period from October to January is considered the peak season across most leisure destinations and demand is likely to further improve during this period. Continued demand growth from the domestic as well as the foreign travel circuits will lead to higher occupancies and rates across all key leisure destinations. We also strongly believe that for the next five years, secondary markets will benefit the most, with improved air connectivity to other cities and the development of national highway infrastructure. With limited room inventory base and very little supply addition, existing hotels in these markets will gain the most.

Hotels positioned between budget and mid-market levels and having an international brand affiliation continue to provide the most attractive opportunities, across most secondary markets. Over the last 12-18 months high growth markets such as Bangalore, Hyderabad and Gurgaon have seen aggressive hotel development activity, and these cities could face a scenario of oversupply in three to four years. A wise strategy for these cities would be to observe the progress of projects under development, as well as demand trends, before an investment decision is taken.

The four main metros and Goa continue to present the best opportunity for luxury hotel development. While these markets have the largest room inventory much commercial development is taking place, especially in the city suburbs. There is a strong positive correlation between hotel demand and commercial development, and factors such as airline seat capacity expansion, growing number of domestic budget airlines and improved frequency will further enhance demand from the transient and airline market segments.

A keen observer of the hotel market would agree that India has been guilty of following a herd mentality when it comes to hotel locations. Almost all development strategies are directed towards projects in the main city centre of high growth markets. Over the next three to five years, the biggest surge in demand is expected to come from commercial zones that are being developed in metro suburbs and secondary markets. This provides a unique opportunity for hotels.

Areas such as Whitefield in Bangalore, Navi Mumbai, Manesar near Gurgaon, the International Airport commercial zone in Hyderabad, Rajarhat and Salt Lake City in Kolkata, Kharadi and Kalyani Nagar in Pune, and the Ahmedabad-Ghandinagar highway will witness large levels of commercial development and are attractive locations for new hotel projects. The lead time for developing a hotel project in India is approximately 24-36 months and it is important to understand the commercial development trends in a market.

Mixed-use development projects that include a hotel, retail and commercial space have gained momentum in the last 24 months and will continue to be an attractive option for developments in large land parcels. Key tourist destinations, such as Jaipur and other cities of historical importance in Rajasthan, Himachal Pradesh, Goa and Kerala will witness integrated tourism projects. The relatively newer concept of weekend travel is poised to gain further momentum with a growing economy and higher disposable incomes, and leisure destinations in close proximity to metro cities will benefit from this trend.

Moreover, the developments and expansions planned in the IT and ITeS segments remain encouraging. The entry of new companies, typically, generates significant room night demand during the start-up period, as processes are set up and executives travel for training. This category of hotel customer ensures a relatively strong base of demand due to a comparatively higher average length of stay. In most hotel markets, insufficient availability and high room rates create conditions that are not conducive for large international conferences to be held. Logistical bottlenecks in these markets also pose a problem. Post 2007, once several markets see an increase in supply, most hotels would adopt an aggressive marketing strategy.

In India, as in other markets across the world, large additions to room supply in hotels calls for investments worth millions of dollars. Availability of finance for funding hotel projects has, traditionally, been an important area of concern. However, promising demand conditions and the industry's strong growth potential has radically changed the way most financial institutions, banks and foreign investment funds look at India today. In the last six months, HVS International has had the opportunity to interact with the representatives of at least twelve foreign investment funds, and we believe that finance is no longer a big issue for a viable project in a good location.

Hotel management companies and international brands are also open to considering equity participation in projects, opening new opportunities for the industry. The outlook for the hospitality market in India is optimistic and will continue to remain so, in our opinion. The economy's buoyancy, initiatives to improve infrastructure, growth in the aviation and real estate sectors and easing of restrictions on foreign investment and, perhaps, most importantly, efforts to make peace with neighbouring Pakistan will fuel demand for hotels across star categories in the majority of markets.

India's hotel industry is increasingly being viewed as investment-worthy, both within the country and outside, and several international chains are keen to establish or enhance their presence here. Over the next three to five years, India will emerge as one of the world's fastest growing tourism markets and will be hard to ignore.

16

VISION FOR THE FUTURE

More than 4,000 surveys were sent to hospitality industry leaders worldwide. Some 500 responses were received from hospitality industry CEOs, corporate executives, and general managers based in three regions: the Americas; Asia/Pacific; and Europe, the Middle East, India and Africa (EMEIA). The Hospitality 2000 study examines five key areas the market, products, organisation, capital and technology. In this period of global transition, these factors will not only define success, but will influence the very ability of hotel organisations to survive in coming years.

The Hospitality 2000 study sends a clear signal that the industry will need to shift its primary focus in the future from the physical assets (the hotels it owns and manages) to the industry's virtual assets (its customers). And this view is by no means supported by just a slim majority—it is held by industry executives around the world by a margin of five to one. If this shift in focus from assets to customers does in fact take place, it will clearly drive great change in the industry, with broad implications for every aspect of the hospitality business.

The traditional "marketplace" will be greatly expanded to incorporate virtual, customer-focused activities to be known as the "marketspace" a completely reconfigured market context and environment that will allow for the delivery of an array of products and services, some traditional, others less so. For those responsible for marketing success in the future, this shift has two important implications.

Currently, revenue per available room (known to industry insiders as REVPAR) is a widely accepted metric for hotel success, reflecting the yield from physical assets (the occupancy and pricing of the guest room). As the customer more clearly becomes the strategic focus, the industry will find that REVPAC (revenue per available customer) will become a key measure of performance.

Industry executives indicate that usage and access to global distribution systems (GDS) will be an important strategy in the future. But there will also be a need to integrate data generated at the property level with reservations systems and corporate information in a total system solution that provides for data warehouses and networked communications. Technology thus supports the shift from a primary focus on reserving the physical room, to better understanding and serving a broad array of customer wants and needs.

The Market

As the hospitality industry considers its future beyond the year 2000, we can be assured of continuing change in the marketplace, although executives surveyed globally varied widely in their views. Not surprisingly, lifestyle and demographic changes are likely to have dramatic impact on the market trends of the future, but regional differences revealed in the Hospitality 2000 study abound. The globalisation of world business and lifestyles -and the growing number of international travellers—will be major forces in marketing hospitality products in the year 2000 and beyond.

Most executives surveyed, regardless of geographic location, believe leisure travel will significantly outperform the business travel segment in the future. While leisure and business travel are expected to achieve growth, the meetings market - including associations, corporate, and social groups - is not forecast to grow and may even experience a slight decline in demand. Planners of convention centres and convention hotels, therefore, need to carefully consider the implications of these findings. The following lifestyle and demographic factors will have a strong impact on the marketing of hospitality products in the future.

Percentage of Respondents in Agreement

	Americas	EMEIA	Asia/Pacific
Baby Boomers	82%	29%	40%
International Travellers	61%	87%	92%
Active Retirees	60%	64%	50%
Increased Wealth	42%	51%	81%
Increased Leisure Time	54%	61%	62%

Customer Purchase Decisions

Reflecting the conventional "locational "bias in the real estate industry, virtually all respondents indicate that location will continue to be the most important influence on the customer's purchase decision, followed by service quality. While less than two-thirds of the respondents indicate that brand affiliation is a strong influence on the purchase decision, 83 percent acknowledge that business travellers will prefer branded products in the future and only two-thirds believe the same about leisure travellers an ambivalence that will undoubtedly be brought into greater focus and reconciled as globalisation continues and branding becomes more prevalent in all types of business.

As to frequent traveller programs—the bane of some companies' marketing existence—only 60 percent of our respondents put much stock in such programs as significant influencers of the buying decision. This is driven quite probably by the fad that these programs are more valuable to the limited number of chains and their customers where there are extensive property networks and customer-tracking systems in place.

Future Marketing Strategies

Essential to marketing strategies is information about guest wants and needs. And yet an overwhelming number of respondents, 93 percent, indicate that they rely on the traditional in-room guest comment card approach to tracking guest satisfaction, a system fraught with weakness principally associated with lack of control and poor response rates from those customers who actually have something important to say. It is encouraging to note that the industry's leadership expects to rely more heavily on third-party market research and focus groups as a means of assessing guest needs and satisfaction in the future.

Executives surveyed emphasise three key marketing approaches: increased use of global distribution systems, linking hotel reservation systems to airline and travel agency networks; enhanced yield management techniques; and service improvements designed to increase guest satisfaction.

Of the growth strategies ranked by executives, strategic alliances topped the list, followed by mergers and acquisitions. Joint ventures, franchising, and management contracts followed in importance. Not surprisingly, new development the most capital-intensive and time-consuming of the growth strategies - is at the bottom of the list in the Americas.

The Product

Decisions about hotel products must be seen through the

lens of changing customer demands—current and future - with an understanding that they are the primary assets of a hotel organisation. The adage—"build it and they will come" no longer applies. Consistent with this philosophy are key findings related to forces driving the building of brand equity. The two major forces cited are:

— The need to increase market share by those companies seeking critical mass; and

— The importance of adapting products to meet the evolving needs of the market due to changing lifestyles and demographics.

As a result of rising customer expectations and the increasing needs of business travellers who wish to take their offices with them when they travel we can expect new product innovations within the guest room, particularly in the area of technology. Eighty percent of industry executives recognise that increased capital will need to be spent on technology upgrades in the hotel room. Anecdotally, however, there seems to be some ambivalence as to whether business travellers want their office setups in the room or downstairs in the more sociable atmosphere of the business centre.

Historically, food and beverage operations have contributed significantly to the industry's revenues, and yet they have also been viewed with mixed feelings by the hoteliers responsible for delivering the profits. The conventional wisdom has frequently been that "the real money is in the rooms." Themed restaurants are also popular among respondents, reflecting the continuing convergence of the entertainment and hospitality industries. This is a trend of great significance and one that truly responds to the customers' focus on collecting experiences as much as material goods.

Organisation

In the future, a customer focus (both internal and external) will imbue business decisions at all levels of the hospitality organisation. Seventy percent see global hotel chains as growing the fastest in the future. While change is occurring at an unprecedented rate, the Hospitality 2000 survey results indicate that visioning for the future is not always on the minds of many of the industry's executives. As the hospitality industry changes, recruitment of skilled management will be critical. Eight out of ten industry executives agree that the ability to recruit experienced management personnel will be an important human resource challenge.

Capital

If current trends are anything to go by, the competition for capital is likely to increase steadily in the future. In response, hospitality companies will need to focus on enhancing shareholder wealth and producing satisfactory returns. As hospitality companies expand into the global economy, it seems clear from this survey that they will need to seek investment capital outside of the local or traditional framework. The majority of responding executives will be looking to public markets and institutional investors to provide the capital for the industry's future growth.

Other prominent sources are expected to be foreign investors (suggesting a continuing trend to globalisation of capital markets) and the pension fund community—long sought after as a result of its huge capital base. Whether the pension funds can overcome their traditional ambivalence about real estate generally and their sharp views about the complexity of the hotel "business" remains to be seen. But on the public markets front, the actual evidence is clear. Securitisation of the hotel industry is well underway, at least in the United States, and is likely to continue to expand in the future.

Impact of Technology

The 21st century will bring the era of the fully-automated hotel, connecting the customer to a universe of diverse products and services offered by an array of providers. Clearly, technology is widely viewed as a means to enhance and facilitate service, but not as an alternative to providing quality service. While there has been speculation that technological innovation may reduce business travel, there is little support for this view among executives surveyed. While over one-half explicitly disagree with such a view, close to one-quarter do not take a position one way or the other.

BIBLIOGRAPHY

Abbey, James R. *Hospitality Sales and Advertising*. Lansing: Educational Institute of the American Hotel and Motel Association, 1998.

American Hotel and Motel Association, Educational Institute. *Hospitality Skills Training Series*. East Lansing: The Institute, 1995.

Anderson, Kenneth. *International Menu Speller*. New York: Wiley, 1993.

Angelo, Rocco M. *An Introduction to Hospitality Today*. Orlando: Educational Institute, American Hotel & Motel Association, 1998.

Baucom, Alfred H. *Hospitality Design for the Graying Generation: Meeting the Needs of a Growing Market*. New York: Wiley, 1996.

Bellucci, Elio C. *The Hospitality Law Desk Reference*. Miami: Southern Beverage Journal, 1994.

Boella, Michael John. *Principles of Hospitality Law*. London: Cassell, 1999.

Brown, Douglas Robert. *The Restaurant Managers Handbook: How to Set Up, Operate, and Manage a Financially Successful Restaurant*. Lauderhill, Atlantic Pub., 1991.

Carmouche, Rita. *Behavioural Studies in Hospitality Management*. New York: Chapman & Hall, 1995.

Eberts, Marjorie. *Careers in Travel, Tourism, and Hospitality*. Lincolnwood: VGM Career Horizons, 1997.

Gee, Chuck Y. *International Hotels: Development and Management*. East Lansing: Educational Institute of the American Hotel & Motel Association, 1994.

Go, Frank M. *Human Resource Management in the Hospitality Industry.* New York: Wiley, 1996.

Goldblatt, Joe Jeff. *Special Events: Best Practices in Modern Event Management.* New York: Van Nostrand Reinhold, 1997.

Hinkin, Timothy R. *Cases in Hospitality Management: A Critical Incident Approach.* New York: Wiley, 1995.

Kavanaugh, Raphael R. *Supervision in the Hospitality Industry.* East Lansing: Educational Institute of the American Hotel & Motel Association, 1995.

Kazarian, Edward A. *Foodservice Facilities Planning.* New York: Van Nostrand Reinhold, 1989.

Kim, Il-Sun Yang. *Inventory Control Systems in Foodservice Organizations: Programmed Study Guide.* Ames: Iowa State University Press, 1992.

Kudrle, Albert E. Public *Relations for Hospitality Managers: Communicating for Greater Profits.* New York: Wiley, 1995.

INDEX

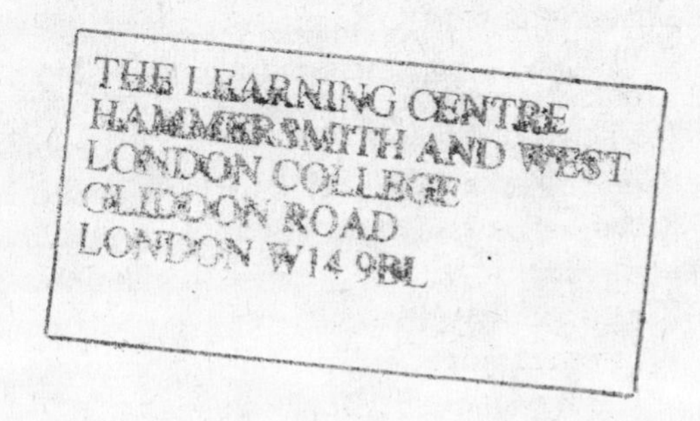